Throughout
all manner of things

Throughout
all manner of things

Sailing around Britain
on
Bella Rosa

JEAN TYRRELL

Copyright © 2015 by Jean Tyrrell

All rights reserved.

No part of this book may be reproduced in any form or by any electronic or mechanical means including information storage and retrieval systems, without permission in writing from the author. The only exception is by a reviewer, who may quote short excerpts in a review.

Paperback ISBN – 978-1-910667-54-5

.epub ISBN – 978-1-910667-56-9

.mobi ISBN – 978-1-910667-55-2

*This book is dedicated to my lovely
husband the Admirable Bob, who has been truly
admirable not only while sailing round Britain with me
as my first mate, but in all aspects of our life together, and
our daughters Sophie and Gracie for being
generally blooming marvellous.*

Foreword

This book started life as a blog and then evolved into an account of all my early experiences in learning how to sail and the big challenge of sailing round Britain.

I decided to transform the blog into a book because I hope that the work I've put into writing it might succeed in raising money for a relevant charity.

No charity could be more relevant to us than the Royal National Lifeboat Institute. It's for this reason that I intend to donate all proceeds from the sale of this book to them. Knowing that the RNLI were always on hand gave us a constant feeling of security, and their advice at various points in our trip was invaluable. Huge thanks to those brave volunteers who are on call twenty four hours a day to look after all of us who venture out into British waters. Also, if you're reading this it means you've been generous enough to buy the book, so a huge thanks to you as well. I hope you enjoy it!

Introduction

In the summer of 2012, along with my husband Bob as first mate, I successfully skippered our boat *Bella Rosa* round mainland Britain. To many people, this voyage might have been nothing special, but as we'd both taken up sailing later in life it was always going to be quite a challenge. Male sailors we met along the way immediately assumed Bob was in charge and either looked on me with pity or ignored me totally. Women offered huge amounts of sympathy as if I'd been dragged along against my better judgment. When Bob told them to direct all technical banter in my direction because I was in charge, they invariably keeled over in disbelief and shock. Outwardly, I smiled sweetly while twiddling the nearest bit of sailing paraphernalia, but, inwardly, I relished those moments and felt my innards do triple somersaults of deep and delicious, triumphant joy!

After years of being obsessed with all things to do with the salty seaside, and admiring all manner of boats from the safety of solid land, I knew that the time had come to actually get myself on a proper cruising yacht, to check out whether it was as fun-filled and adventurous as it appeared to be. I was approaching fifty when I was overcome by the need finally to have a go at learning how to sail. Actually, it wasn't my age as such that had much to do with it. If anything, a gentle activity that would soothe the senses, like antique appreciation classes, would have been more appropriate, rather than opting for something that I subsequently discovered could be dangerous, was often tiring and was always unpredictable.

Always one to believe that if a job is worth doing it's worth doing properly, it was clear that the place to start was with some sort of training and instruction. I had no intention of being a nautical liability to myself and the world at large. Over the following few years, I put myself through a whole series of courses and exams that would enable me not only to be useful on a boat but capable of skippering it too!

From the first moment I decided to try sailing, I became obsessed with all things 'boaty'. In fact, I was in grave danger of becoming a mighty 'boat bore'. There was so much more to sailing than I'd previously imagined. There were boat shows to go to, books on all aspects of sailing to read, land-based theory courses and hands-on practical courses. Along with basic sailing skills, you could learn about sea survival with real sound effects in real water and how to operate a ship's radio. There were radar operating skills to be acquired and diesel engine workshops to be attended. Prior to becoming interested in boats, I wouldn't have thought anything could more boring than attending a diesel engine workshop, but this was going to be different. It was to do with engines that were connected to boats and therefore connected to the sea and therefore would be *soooo* relevant and engaging. As important as anything, of course, being involved in 'serious' yachting would provide me with a legitimate excuse to buy one of those candy-striped pink and white rugby shirts from Crew. There were also going to be many other new and equally exciting shopping opportunities.

I went to the Southampton Boat Show and padded on and off beautifully appointed yachts, coveting them all in an overwhelming mental haze of desire. I smiled mysteriously at the salesmen, most of whom clearly assumed that I'd taken a wrong turning on the pedestrian walkway in the multi-storey and was really looking for the main entrance to the Southampton John Lewis. "I'd like one of these," I said to one of the salesmen on a brand new 34-foot Beneteau. He chuckled patronisingly and suggested that I should try a Greek flotilla holiday first. I'd really like that man to know that we ended up choosing a bigger and better Swedish boat, so, *neeerrr*.

I started to read as many books about boat handling as possible, took out a subscription to *Yachting Monthly*, and eventually signed up for even more courses to do with the finer details of navigation and boat handling. I discovered Libby Purves' account of sailing round Britain with her young family but it was when I was midway through Jonathan Raban's account of single-handedly sailing round Britain that it dawned on me that sailing round Britain was what I wanted to end up doing. Britain was here, right on our very own doorstep, and was just begging to be sailed round … by me.

Up to this point, Bob had shown little interest in sailing, and was concentrating his efforts on learning the guitar, fishing and playing tennis. I badly needed him if I was going to be able to avoid having to do my circumnavigation with a bevy of unknown gap-year youths on one of those organised expeditions called things like 'Non-Stop GB' or 'Britain or Bust'.

There were several things to consider if this whole operation was going to work out in a favourable way (at least to me). Never being one willingly to take orders from anyone else without getting shirty and argumentative, I'd have to get myself up to a standard good enough to be the one in charge, stay ahead in terms of qualifications and experience, and get Bob motivated and trained up to a good enough standard to be of use. The getting Bob motivated part was no mean feat but, after some pressure, a bit of emotional blackmail and a promise that the guitar could come with us, he finally agreed to accompany me, and started to take the necessary courses to become a good, obedient and useful crew member.

In the space of a couple of years, we both had some decent sailing certificates glued into the back of our RYA log books, had bought our own boat (not a Beneteau 34), had sailed it back from Holland by ourselves and had spent the subsequent time getting as much practice as possible dealing with the British tides and the hugely variable British weather. We also fell hopelessly in love with *Bella Rosa*, our lovely new 37-foot Swedish sailing boat.

The process of accumulating experience with and without guidance proved to be quite eventful. It wasn't just about dealing with the boat; we encountered many 'interesting characters' along the way. We took many calculated risks, made some bold decisions and probably did a whole load of daft things as well. We must have got away with it because we're still here and *Bella Rosa* is still in one piece and continuing to live happily in Lymington.

We suspected that many of our friends thought that we were crazy to attempt even to leave the Solent after only a few years' experience, but we felt that with careful planning, patience and due respect for weather conditions we should eventually get all the way round Britain. Failing that, we could park up somewhere close by, where none of our friends or family were likely to go, and keep a low profile for the three months. If we sandpapered our faces in order to look convincingly weathered and got a job lot of cheap tartan souvenirs to distribute on our 'return' no one would be any the wiser. It probably wouldn't be long before we started to believe the story ourselves.

Many friends were puzzled why we would ever want to subject ourselves to British coastal conditions, even for a week, let alone three months, especially when places like the Mediterranean were easily accessible via a quick charter flight and flotilla. Many suggested that we should forget trying to do it in one go and consider the benefits of doing it in smaller stages with breaks in-between. Our response was that we knew so little of our own country, especially the most northern parts, and we wanted to see it all in one go without losing momentum. We also desperately wanted it to be more of a real challenge rather than a series of short 'holidays'. This was to be a step (or a sail) into the unknown.

We could have gone by road but, since discovering sailing, we were now in a position to see all that we wanted to see from the sea and arrive from the sea while avoiding roads and traffic jams. Good fish and chips would be constantly available, and no one would try to pass off ouzo as an acceptable drink. A massive advantage of staying local would be that, even if we were to experience frequent hostile weather and remote and exposed stretches of difficult seas, a faulty engine, a stuck mainsail or a Force 10 gale just around the corner, there would also be a fighting chance of being fully understood on the ship's radio, even in the Glasgow region. One more outstandingly positive point was that after we'd left our port of departure, Lymington, we knew that all we needed to do was to keep turning right and we'd surely end up back where we'd started at some point in the near future. There were so many plus points in favour of circumnavigating the British mainland that sailing the Mediterranean was never on the cards.

Our eventual trip round Britain was the most amazing physical, mental, emotional and cultural experience, and we loved every nook and cranny of it. From the decks of *Bella Rosa* we were able to bond with so many of our island communities and observe the true nature of our homeland. We felt so lucky to have Britain as our home. We'd allowed ourselves twelve weeks to do the trip in order to give ourselves plenty of time to stop and explore places, as well as to allow for the inevitable days (and odd week!) being stormbound in port. We felt we were extraordinarily lucky to have the opportunity to be able to do what we did, and felt frequently exhilarated by the experience. To say that we were pretty pleased with our achievement is an understatement, but we were also strongly aware that much of the credit for the success of our mission should go to *Bella Rosa*, the Wonder Boat. There's talk that she's bringing out her own book soon entitled *An Intelligent Yacht's Guide to Circumnavigating Britain with a Couple of Unexceptional Humans.*

There's one other thing to say about this adventure: the older you get, the more you realise that few things in life ever really get completed. Parenthood, marriage, friendship, work, learning and even shopping (or especially shopping!) rarely have clear beginnings and endings, and so, as well as their joys, they have their frustrations too. The clichéd but apposite way of saying this is that life is a process. The odd and surprising thing about circumnavigating Britain was how the geographical completion of the journey– arriving exactly where we'd left off – was such a profound completion in other ways too. We arrived home and there was literally nothing we regretted, nothing more we could have asked for and no corner left unturned. It was satisfying on every level. There aren't many experiences in life about which you can say that.

The Route

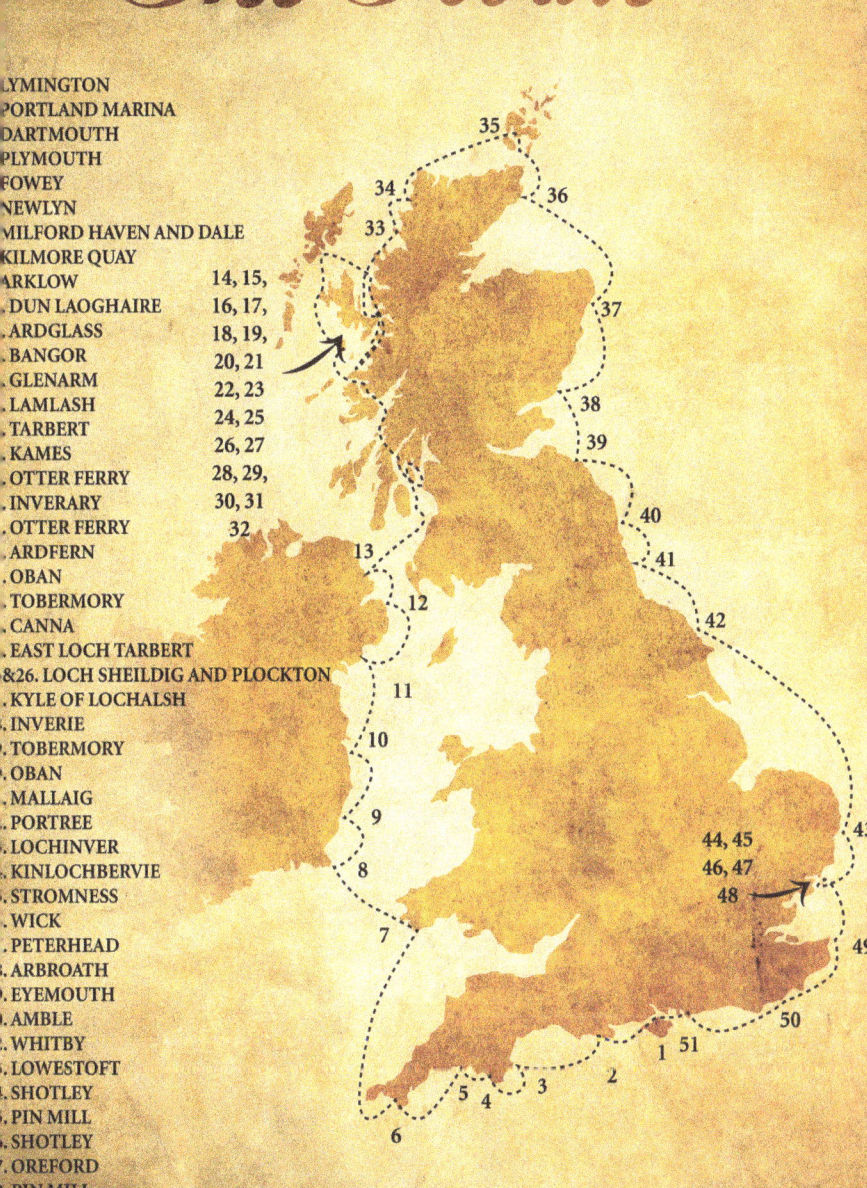

- LYMINGTON
- PORTLAND MARINA
- DARTMOUTH
- PLYMOUTH
- FOWEY
- NEWLYN
- MILFORD HAVEN AND DALE
- KILMORE QUAY
- ARKLOW
- DUN LAOGHAIRE
- ARDGLASS
- BANGOR
- GLENARM
- LAMLASH
- TARBERT
- KAMES
- OTTER FERRY
- INVERARY
- OTTER FERRY
- ARDFERN
- OBAN
- TOBERMORY
- CANNA
- EAST LOCH TARBERT
- &26. LOCH SHEILDIG AND PLOCKTON
- KYLE OF LOCHALSH
- INVERIE
- TOBERMORY
- OBAN
- MALLAIG
- PORTREE
- LOCHINVER
- KINLOCHBERVIE
- STROMNESS
- WICK
- PETERHEAD
- ARBROATH
- EYEMOUTH
- AMBLE
- WHITBY
- LOWESTOFT
- SHOTLEY
- PIN MILL
- SHOTLEY
- OREFORD
- PIN MILL
- RAMSGATE
- EASTBOURNE
- ITCHENOR

14, 15, 16, 17, 18, 19, 20, 21, 22, 23, 24, 25, 26, 27, 28, 29, 30, 31, 32

Incompetent Crew

I was approaching fifty fast, and feeling a little restless, as you do when it suddenly occurs to you that life isn't going to go on forever. If it was a case of do or die, the die part had inconveniently moved to the end of the tunnel where the light used to be. Fifty is definitely a time to crack on with those lurking, unfulfilled ambitions before it becomes physically and mentally inadvisable to leave the house unaccompanied.

Men are known to deal with hitting midlife by doing things to help convince themselves they're still the stud they always thought they were. This usually means buying a heavy duty motorbike or running off with a young woman called Svetlana. As a woman, and therefore disinterested in all things metal or called Svetlana (unless she could do the ironing enthusiastically), it wasn't an ego boost I was after. I just fancied trying something new and adventurous, maybe with the potential of a tiny risk factor to add a little frisson of excitement. Both daughters had fled the nest, and I was ready, willing and available. I waited for spiritual guidance.

Once I'd made the decision to look for a suitable challenge, it was remarkable how quickly the solution came to me. I woke up one morning feeling like I was channelling Sir Frances Chichester. The voice in my head said authoritatively, "You will learn to sail and must ring the RYA today and sign up for a course." There was no question about it; I felt commanded by powers unknown to book myself on to the all ladies Competent Crew course, which was leaving from Portsmouth in three days' time.

I went out to purchase a flashy, leopard-skin-print top to have on hand if we were to venture ashore of an evening.

My only previous experience of sailing had been a two-day Introduction to Sailing taster session with Bob twenty years previously. Getting food poisoning within eight hours of setting off meant that the only detail I could really remember well was the interior of the ladies public toilets in Cowes. The sailing part of that weekend remains a blur. Understandably, the experience had put me off going on another boat for some time, which was why it took the full twenty years to rekindle my interest and sign up for the five-day sailing course I was about to embark upon now. Despite the dismal memory of the taster weekend, I've always loved the sea, always loved looking at boats, and have always felt that the two would match up very nicely. I was desperate to like sailing and was ready to give it another go.

Before I set off, I had no idea whether I would love or hate being on a sailing course. I was heading into unknown territory and was worried that I might find the experience fairly uncomfortable and may even suffer from seasickness. However, I promised myself that I would embrace any discomfort and misery with the open acceptance of a Buddhist monk. I would not let myself whinge, get bored, impatient or irritable, feel regretful or demand to be let off at the nearest convenient port. Disconcertingly unlike other types of weekend workshops, it's not possible to do a runner that easily from a yacht. Most of the time, escape would involve swimming for it and, with the strong tides in the Solent, enduring the course would probably turn out to be a lot less painful than being swept out into the English Channel and dying from hypothermia or being run down by a supertanker. I was going to be my best and positive self. It was meant to be a challenge, after all. I would wait until I was back on dry land to decide whether I loved it or hated it but, ultimately, it didn't matter because at last I was giving it a go.

I'd reassured myself that at least part of the course was bound to be sitting comfortably on the polished teak deck, floating gently along in the sun with a glass of crisp white wine in hand. With that in mind, I wondered if it might turn out to be quite fun or even become a passion. I was brought down to earth with a bump on the morning of departure for Portsmouth when I somehow managed to get the index finger of my right hand trapped in the car door. This was very unfortunate, not only because I am right-handed but also because, as I was to discover, the index finger is involved in virtually every activity on a boat that isn't sitting on deck with a glass of wine in hand. As it happens, sitting on deck with a glass of wine in hand while sailing proved – disappointingly – not to be on the Competent Crew course syllabus at all.

Our instructor was Karen, who has since, despite our constant efforts to turn her into a gibbering wreck, gone on to become head of training at Sunsail. This is a well-deserved position, as she was brilliant. Other than Karen, there were two other ladies: Clarissa and Julie. There were three cabins and four of us, and the skipper naturally had one of the cabins to herself, being higher up the pecking order. Karen told us to sort out the remaining cabin situation among ourselves but, by the time I'd registered that I needed to make my move, the other two were already installed in the two vacant cabins and were unpacking furiously. There was, however, an advantage to sleeping in the public thoroughfare of the yacht, otherwise known as the saloon, and that was being in close proximity to the loo and the kettle, which, as I was approaching fifty, was a comfort.

Karen was a bubbly blonde from Barnsley, and was a highly experienced yachtswoman. She had captain status, and therefore had the authority to marry people at sea. With it being an all-ladies week, I couldn't foresee any weddings taking place, but life can be full of surprises. I was beginning to regret not having brought something a little more dressy to wear, but there was always the leopard-skin-print top.

Clarissa was in her early twenties, and had arrived with a large Australian in tow, who turned out to be her boyfriend. He wasn't coming with us; he was merely delivering Clarissa to her sailing fate, and was the wrong sex for this particular course anyway. Clarissa's boyfriend had aspirations to skipper a super yacht, and wanted Clarissa to familiarise herself with boats, so that she could join him as a hostess on a super yacht. Given that Clarissa had never done anything remotely outdoorsy before, he'd suggested she might gain experience on a Competent Crew course. I personally couldn't see any similarities between a 37-foot overblown tub with one loo and a Calor gas cooker, and a luxury motor yacht the size of Harrods, with cream leather upholstery, vast sunbathing decks and a dedicated champagne fridge. Perhaps the sheer contrast would make wielding trays of drinks on a super yacht seem like a dream job and make Clarissa feel eternally indebted to her Australian. It was an ingenious tactic on his part, I thought.

Julie was a velvet-head-banded army wife, who was doing the more advanced Day Skipper qualification. This involved knowing a certain amount of theory beforehand. She had sailed a lot on the family boat, but apparently had no qualifications at all in anything, not even O levels, as it turned out. She wanted to feel like she could be seen to be successful at something, and gain some sort of qualification to prove it, and thought that she stood a fighting chance with sailing. Her husband was apparently captain of the army skiing team, captain of the army sailing team and, by the sound of it, nauseatingly good at everything, which must have compounded her feelings of uselessness. If it had been down to me, I would have ditched him pronto and started again, but there's no denying the enduring spirit of the army wife. I was the oldest by a good fifteen years, and hoped – along with the bad finger – that I would be able to use these things to my advantage. We all had very different starting points, but our common objective was to learn to sail and enjoy the process. Julie was the only one that wasn't a teeny bit scared out of the three of us.

It wasn't long before I discovered that sailing boats can sometimes move along at a sharp angle and, when you change direction, everyone has to move rapidly to the other side of the boat without getting their heads knocked off. The potential for getting your head knocked off is huge, and the body soon adopts a more hunched and cautious pose in response to the threat. The object that's number one on the list of 'things on a boat that might do you damage or shorten your life' is the large, girder-sized metal arm traditionally known as a boom. It constantly hangs over everyone's heads like the sword of Damocles, and it swings from one side to the other each time you change to another tack. It should be under control, but that depends entirely on who is in charge of it. When it's not being swung across the boat, it's still waiting there like a predatory raptor for the chance to either knock you out, give you a hard swipe or, at the very least, a bit of a bruising and a bad headache.

The bigger the boat, the bigger the boom. I was beginning to understand why Clarissa was on the course. Sailing is a lot to do with keeping your head intact. If it got knocked off by the boom on a super yacht, you'd know about it. It was a while before I was allowed to manoeuvre the boom, and several years after returning from the course before my body was able to return to its normal upright position.

To the untrained eye, the workings of a boat look

highly complex, and to the trained eye, they still look complex. There are ropes of different thicknesses and colours everywhere, but they're not called ropes; they're called 'halyards', 'sheets' and 'warps'. The halyards are the ropes that hoist a sail, flag or yard (which is a metal stay on a boat), and, not surprisingly, halyard comes from the term 'haul a yard'. A sheet is a line that controls the moveable corners of a sail and comes from the old English word 'sceata', meaning the lower corner of a sail. A warp is the name of the ropes used to tie the boat up, but refers to a method of moving a boat round when moored.

Modern-day boat-speak is a very distinct language, and most of it goes right back to the dawning of the origins of sailing. Being an island nation with so much contact with and reliance on sailing and the sea, there are a huge number of sailing terms that have become a regular part of everyday conversation. 'Slush fund', for instance, sounds like a really hip city term, but it's nautical. Slush was the grease left over after boiling meat on the ship and the fund was the money they got when they sold it off once back on land. 'Bitter end' is another colloquialism from sailing. A 'bitt' is a post attached to the deck of a ship and, when the rope is paid out to the end, it becomes the bitter end. I was relieved when Karen talked about 'parking', as opposed to mooring, but I think it's because she realised that she was on to a sticky wicket with us lot of amateurs.

I discovered a whole raft of new devices and pieces of equipment that I knew nothing about. There were cleats, shackles, blocks, forestays and backstays. The list was endless. I was, however, in the fortunate and happy position of not being expected to know anything; I was at the very bottom of the sailing hierarchy. I was a blank canvas, waiting expectantly for the brush of knowledge to apply its wide-sweeping strokes of colour to the landscape of my mind (my day job is an artist!). Even if they put the letters 'i' and 'n' in front of the word competent on the certificate at the end of the week, I would still know more than I did at the beginning.

Karen worked us all very hard, but gave us equal attention, and was a deep well of seafaring information. She clearly loved her job, and wanted us to get the best out of the course. As a Day Skipper student, Julie was going to be working on the planning side of things, and Clarissa and I were going to be doing most of the practical support stuff. That is what crewing is all about and, on a serious note, sailing is dangerous not only when a skipper gets things wrong but when the crew can't carry out their sometimes seemingly menial tasks competently. For example, tying a warp (to save you looking back, that's one of the types of rope on a boat) to a cleat requires care and skill if the boat's to be held securely in a wind and if the crew member isn't to lose their fingers.

It's all credit to Karen that she was patient, kind and funny, but firm, and instilled in me an understanding of the responsibilities of sailing whether as captain or crew. We all knew that she wasn't someone you could mess with. I checked around for the plank that you're made to walk if you get out of line. I couldn't see it, but felt it was wise to be cautious and assume that there was a modern, flat-pack version stowed away somewhere on the boat. In normal circumstances, I often have trouble bowing to authority, but in this case I recognised that I needed to be a bit better qualified before instigating a mutiny. I was going to save that for a higher level course. If we'd wanted to shirk, there was nowhere to hide. Our home for five days and nights was a space less than eleven metres by four metres. Skulking was only possible in the guise of making a cup of tea, but the weather was warm and sunny, and we were having fun.

The Solent

The school boat was based at Port Solent, which is roughly four nautical miles up the Portsmouth estuary and situated so close to the M27 that you could have hitched a lift from passing traffic from the deck of the boat. Call me picky, but I can't see the point of having your boat somewhere where you're deafened by traffic and are in danger of inhaling toxic levels of exhaust fumes.

As we made our way up and down the Solent, sailing proved itself to be an absorbing activity. Once the sails were set for a particular course, we sat back in the cockpit and were lulled by the sounds of the hull cutting effortlessly through the water. The sound of sailing is incredibly soothing, and the thought that we were being powered by the wind alone was exhilarating. We took turns on the helm, but for the first part of the week they all laughed at me as I stood rigid with apprehension, feet clamped astride on the deck for support, with knuckles glowing white as I gripped the wheel. By the fourth day, I'd finally got the hang of it and found that I could steer with one foot casually resting upon the cockpit seat and a mug of tea in hand. I'd begun to enjoy steering the boat, and was sure that I liked the whole sailing experience.

There is a plethora of sailing schools based in the Solent area, and you can always tell who is under instruction and who isn't. The school boats hover about, sometimes chucking fenders overboard and then retrieving them. This is not just for the fun of it; the fenders act as a 'man overboard', which is a standard sailing school drill.

I suppose using live volunteers would have contravened health and safety regulations, and a fender would be less likely to threaten to sue. The crew on board school boats often have matching but ill-fitting waterproofs. You can spot the dithery, reluctant students, the puzzled but keen ones and the ones that think they know it all already. We must have been flashing our 'under instruction' status in full, glorious peacock colours, as we struggled to retrieve fenders without falling in, and constantly adjusted our ill-fitting waterproofs. I would probably have put us all in the puzzled but keen category.

The Solent is a very busy waterway so, when you're not focused on tasks on your own boat or keeping a close eye on the activities of the boom, there are plenty of other things to look at. The large commercial ports of Southampton and Portsmouth are situated on the mainland, and there are dozens of smaller, pretty harbours to be found tucked into the coastline on the mainland and the coast of the Isle of Wight. There is a wide range of other boats that regularly use the Solent for both commercial and leisure purposes. Huge, laden container ships come up from the east side of the Solent and make a slow turn in a specially designated 'precautionary' area near Cowes in order to head up to the docks in Southampton Water. Out in open water, these big ships can do impressive speeds of 20 knots or more and, given that the average speed of a small yacht is only about 5 or 6 knots, it's a good idea to keep well out of the way. If you did have an altercation with a cargo ship, you could hardly use the excuse that you didn't see it coming, except perhaps in thick fog.

There are ferries galore criss-crossing from various ports on the mainland to the Isle of Wight and back, and much bigger ferries leaving for destinations further afield, such as France, Spain or the Channel Islands. Some of them go very fast and sometimes it appears that boats are coming at you from all directions. The volumes of close quarter's traffic never worried me with Karen in charge. When under threat, she would narrow her gimlet eyes, check each one out individually, pause briefly and then say, "Right, dip behind that boat there". At the time, it was a total mystery to me how she seemed to know what to do, but it worked like magic every time, and we finished the course intact, so she must have been doing the right thing. I've since learnt that there are certain things called 'rules of the road', and if you adhere to them you can avoid collisions most of the time. Even though I know this now, I still feel that when it all works, and you remain unscathed, it's nothing short of a miracle.

There must be several thousand leisure boats moored in many different marinas bordering the Solent, and the Solent is their local playground. The presence of so many other sailing vessels does make it a particularly precarious place to be, but it also makes it a perfect instruction ground. There are more dangers and lessons to be learnt in the vicinity of coastlines and busy ports than out in the open sea.

The Solent is sandwiched between two coastlines, which provide a large range of hazards you can practise avoiding. There are also tides to consider, and the ones in the Solent can be quite challenging. Karen explained to us that a flood tide (the tide leading up to high water) comes up from the west of the Solent but, sneakily, also comes round the other side of the Isle of Wight shortly afterwards. This confusingly means that there can be two high waters, and this feature is an anomaly, which you find only in a few places where a tide gets split by an island. I sat back and thought how glad I was that I didn't officially need to know any of that stuff in detail, being still a lowly, but now slightly more competent, crew member. Julie went into her puzzled but keen mode and adjusted her waterproofs again.

Karen also told us that the wide range of strengths and heights of tide in the Solent creates a whole range of mooring opportunities, some of which involved mathematical calculations. I went down below to put the kettle on and find the biscuits. I had no inkling at the time but I was going to need to know all about stuff like that at a later date.

We repeated manoeuvres again and again, until Karen felt that we'd got the hang of it. We jumped on to pontoons, tied the boat up, untied the boat, jumped back on the boat, attached the boat to mooring buoys, attached the boat to quay walls, attached the boat to other boats, and some of us (mentioning no names) would have attached it to the nearest pub wall if there had been a pub wall more conveniently situated at the water's edge. Every journey on a boat starts with an unattaching and ends with an attaching, unless you're anchoring, and then you'd still have the prospect of some sort of an attachment at a later stage. Attaching a boat involves knowledge of knots and numerous methods of tying a boat up with a rope.

Learning about knots and securing lines is a major feature of the Competent Crew course. Different methods are used for different situations. At first, I couldn't see how I would ever remember everything, but mnemonic devices are used all the time to help. The one I had the most initial success with was the 'OXO'. To put a rope around a cleat on a pontoon you would do a ring round the cleat, followed by two figures of eight, and finish it off with another ring. Hey presto, the OXO! It's possibly the easiest and most satisfying thing for a novice sailor to learn, and is difficult to misunderstand or forget even if you are a complete moron.

It was a lovely summer and the weather was so warm that we sailed in T-shirts, and slept with all the windows and hatches wide open. The atmosphere was convivial and supportive. We spent the evenings in different pubs at different marinas and, wherever we went, hordes of people would come over to say hello to Karen. It appeared that she'd taught most of Hampshire to sail, and was friends with just about everyone else. The sailing fraternity was a lively lot, and in most cases quite a lot younger than me. I wondered whether to strike up a seafaring conversation with some of the more ancient, weather-bitten types, but decided to stick with the youth. Arriving somewhere attractive and having a buzzy social life is part of sailing, just as après ski is part of skiing. It was a lifestyle that was steadily growing on me.

Halfway through the week, my damaged index finger had started to go spongy and turn a sludge green colour. Miraculously, because of this, I was banned from doing the anchoring procedure. When I saw that this involved hauling up forty metres of heavy chain out of a locker and laying it out on the deck, I knew that the finger trapping had happened for a reason. Later, when Clarissa and I had to prove that we could manoeuvre a dinghy, Karen insisted that I should wear a bright yellow Marigold rubber glove to protect my bad finger. It wasn't the rubber glove that made it difficult to row the dinghy; we were prostrate with laughter. The laughter increased as Clarissa and I tried to get out of the dinghy, both of us being at opposite ends of the size scale. We somehow managed to get the dinghy wedged under the pontoon, but eventually crawled out of it without it tipping up. The dinghy survived the ordeal but has been in therapy ever since.

It was shortly after the dinghy exercise that Karen decided that I needed medical attention for my bad finger. We all set off to Cowes, where there was a health centre that was used to dealing with boat injuries. Although my bad finger hadn't started as a boat injury, it was heading rapidly in the direction of becoming one, as I was finding attaching and unattaching anything increasingly difficult.

I was dropped off, got the finger lanced and bandaged, picked up some antibiotics and was back at the boat in less than an hour. Everything about the Isle of Wight is very 1950s, and that includes the NHS (but all in a good way).

For me, one of the most exciting things on the Competent Crew course was the night sail. Despite Julie's qualification being called *Day* Skipper, a night sail is an important part of the course. It was all down to Julie to deal with the navigation, but we had the privilege of taking part without having any of the responsibility. I couldn't imagine how you could possibly sail at night without a massive floodlight fixed to the front of the boat, but here was my chance to find out. To enable an early and easy start, we attached ourselves to a mooring buoy just outside Yarmouth so that to set off all we had to do was slip off the buoy and we would be away.

With a 2.00 a.m. start the following morning, an early dinner and an early night seemed like a sensible idea. Like a child on Christmas Eve, I was so excited that I didn't fall asleep until 1.00 a.m., only to be woken at 1.30 with a cup of tea ready to get going at 2.00. We put the sail up, slipped off the mooring and slowly made our way east through the dark night. We felt like smugglers, and if ever I had a *Swallows and Amazons* moment, that was it. The only sound was of the boat gently making its way through the water. Julie was working hard, waving around a hand-held compass and identifying different buoys by their lights. At last, the secret of night sailing was out: it's not all done by guesswork; it's done by lights flashing in different sequences to state their presence and identity.

We sailed on until night became morning, dropped an anchor in a shallow part of the bay and celebrated the success of our adventure with sausage and bacon rolls and coffee.

Our five-day course with Karen was one of endless laughs but a lot of serious learning and bag loads of practice. Karen had the ability to get us to do exactly what she wanted without ruffling any feathers. She judged us perfectly – the mark of an expert teacher.

Julie got her well-deserved Day Skipper certificate, and was deliriously happy that this was the first serious thing she felt she'd ever achieved. We were all almost as emotional about it as she was. Clarissa admitted that she had experienced her first extreme sport adrenalin rush ever when she helmed the boat in 15 knots of wind at eight nautical miles an hour. She was truly converted to a life of fresh air and adventure. I was thrilled with the whole experience, I found that I loved life on the water, but knew that I still had a huge amount to learn, and was now geared up to take it further. My plan was to look into doing the Day Skipper theory course. Karen was still in good humour, and was genuinely happy for us when she handed over our various certificates. On the way home, the idea of getting more experience and becoming much better qualified was taking a good strong hold, but never for a minute at that stage did I think I would ever be a skipper.

Day Skipper Theory

After successfully completing the Competent Crew course, I was highly motivated to learn more about the navigational side of sailing. I wasn't sure at this stage how I was going to get myself on to another yacht, but I wanted to be well prepared in case an opportunity presented itself.

I was unlikely to find any opportunities in Britain to get more sailing experience – even as a lowly crew member – but I pricked up my ears when I heard that you didn't necessarily need a lot of experience to go on a flotilla holiday in the Mediterranean. There are minimal tides for a start, and there is always a lead team to give you guidance and save a parking place for you at the end of the day. The idea of going on a flotilla somewhere warm with a backup team of skilled sailors was very tempting, and sailing experience to Day Skipper level was apparently sufficient enough to be able to be in charge of a boat. With this goal in mind, I signed up for a Day Skipper theory evening class in Bristol and, when I'd finished that, would find a Day Skipper practical course. The fact that I got horribly lost on the way home after the first session made me wonder whether, in reality, I had the navigational skills of a daddy-long-legs, but Rome wasn't built in a day. Before long, I could not only effectively find my way home from Bristol but could navigate myself round my own kitchen table with aplomb. It was all beginning to look very hopeful.

The main piece of equipment we needed for navigation, apart from the charts, was something called a Portland Plotter. I discovered that a plotter is not a device used to unblock a sink, but a plastic, ruler-like instrument with a swivelling wheel with compass positions on it. You use it to find out which compass course you need to follow to get from one place to another. The most important thing about using the plotter was to get the arrow pointing in the direction you wanted to travel.

It was surprising how easy it was to make that small but critical error, which would then throw all calculations out of the window and have you heading for certain death, when all you wanted to do was reach a secluded cove for a pleasant but simple lunch.

This was all in theory, of course, and at this stage a theoretical shipwreck on a dangerous rocky outcrop wasn't going to have life-changing consequences. The thought that a mistake like that could happen in a real life navigational situation could, however, put a lot of people off ever venturing out on a yacht in the first place. In my case, it was hard to imagine a real life navigational situation with me in charge, so I carried on regardless, honing my Portland Plotter skills on the kitchen table.

I was expecting navigational theory to be quite tedious, but it's not all drawing lines on charts and fiddling with the Portland Plotter. For example, you need to know what to do in an emergency. I hadn't realised there were so many things that could go wrong. When they do go wrong, you have to spring into action, because you're surrounded by fathoms of water, and help is not necessarily at hand. There may not be enough time to search for your reading glasses in order to read the instruction manual on how to launch the life raft when your boat is already semi-submerged, so you need to know that stuff beforehand. Getting only as far as page two in the instruction manual is not advisable when dealing with the ocean. For starters, there is an official script to be used when you radio a May Day call. They need to know specifics, like whereabouts in the ocean you are. There aren't street names and pubs to identify your position. If a helicopter has to come to winch you to safety, you need to know that clipping the winching line on to the boat could end badly.

A lot of navigation is about identifying where you are, and this is where things like buoys come in. We learnt all about the different types of buoys and the lights they show at night. We learnt that they can denote an area of dangerous rocks or can mark an entry channel. We learnt that it's best not to crash into them, and sometimes they can get dragged out of place by a tide. Buoys can be your best friends out at sea or coming into harbours, and lighthouses are your guardian angels. When you are near land, there are various ways to identify where you are, from recognising headland shapes to spotting conspicuous buildings like churches or towers. To find the way into the main channel at Portsmouth, you line up a specific war memorial with the edge of a specific block of flats, and follow this transit in until you arrive at a certain buoy, when you then change direction. All this worked well on paper, and it was all beginning to make much more sense.

The Day Skipper theory course took two terms of once-a-week visits to Bristol to complete, and I was completely amazed that I enjoyed every minute. I passed the Day Skipper theory exam, somehow managed to get everything right, stuck the certificate in my log book, and felt armed and ready for the open sea. All I needed to do was find the right Day Skipper practical course with the right instructor, and this time I was going to make sure I had a cabin of my own! One small problem was that Bob still wasn't showing much interest in sailing, and I had a feeling that I was going to need him to be interested.

Day Skipper Practical

It was at our Day Skipper theory certificate presentation evening while quaffing a glass of sherry that I was introduced to a man who ran his own sailing school. "Why would I choose to do the practical course with you and not Sunsail?" I asked. He told me that he was the only sailing school he knew that offered gourmet food and let people have their own cabin. I thought back to the cheap sausages we'd had on my Competent Crew course, the slightly too open-plan accommodation, and considered the sheer luxury of having my own cosy cabin. I would seriously miss doing a further qualification with Karen, but it was the prospect of excellent food and having a cabin to myself that swung the decision in favour of this instructor.

Prior to fixing a date for the course, I had to do something to stimulate Bob's interest in sailing. It came in the form of a day out with some old friends, Richard and Sue Owen, who not only knew one end of a boat from the other, they actually owned one of their own. We met them down in Poole Harbour and sailed out with Bob helming under the watchful eye of Richard. If you ever sail with anyone better than Richard for exuding calm, encouragement and trust that you're safe, I'd like to meet them. We had a fabulous day: a perfect amount of wind to get a sensation of what a boat feels like heeling gently on a close reach while carving through the water. When we anchored in Studland Bay for a delicious lunch with wine, I sensed Bob was beginning to see the merits of combining an outdoor experience with a constant sea view, the ability to go quite fast while sitting down, having lunch on deck and being away from the horrible hoards. "It's not always like that," I said. "Sometimes, there's no wind, sometimes there's too much, and sometimes there's no wine." I said no more after that because I didn't want to put him off.

After some persuasion, Bob eventually agreed to come with me to do the Competent Crew course while I did my Day Skipper practical. It would be just the two of us being instructed by the same person (the man I'd met), but I still insisted on having my own cabin.

To say that the aforementioned instructor ran a sailing school was a bit of an overstatement. On arrival at the marina where he was based, it was soon apparent that he was the only person involved. We went down the pontoon to his berth, and there he was on deck, all 5 feet of him, bare chested and revealing that he had more hair on his body than his head. I don't like to judge by appearances and, in any case, I thought to myself, being able to look down on your teacher might turn out to have its advantages. He seemed very enthusiastic, professed to like good food, and didn't give any indication at the time of having height issues.

I'm not going to be specific about who this person is or where the 'sailing school' is, because, following our 'feedback session' at the end of the course, he may have made friends with his inner child, and we wouldn't want to compromise his progress at becoming a nicer person. However, if you are ever considering signing up for a sailing course, remember to ask specifically about the quality of food. If you hear the word 'gourmet', and the person saying it is unusually short, you will know what to do.

We set off from this small marina situated near a well-known, picturesque resort in Devon. During the course, I was to do all the navigation, and Bob was to learn all the same practical stuff that Karen had taught me. The intention was to head east towards Salcombe, stop in some small places on the way, and then head back again five days later. I'm going to give our instructor the pseudonym 'Nobby' to avoid the potential prospect of him recognising himself and subsequently stalking me with a meat cleaver. In any case, he turned out to be a complete knob so, as far as I'm concerned, the name seems very appropriate.

Day 1 went well enough but, as we settled down for our dinner, it turned out that Nobby's idea of a gourmet meal was a chunk of anything meat-like, covered in a jar of 'Chicken Tonight'. No wonder he said that he took charge of all the cooking; he only had to open a jar and switch the oven on. Chicken Tonight is obviously a perfectly acceptable convenience food if there's nothing fresh to hand, but this was a clear case of misrepresentation, as by no stretch of the imagination could it be classified as gourmet. I've looked it up just to confirm that I wasn't doing the jar of Chicken Tonight an injustice. Gourmet is, as I previously understood, characterised by refined, even elaborate, preparations of high-quality, exotic ingredients. Perhaps he should have hidden the jar and encouraged us to go for an aperitif while he prepared the meal. Who knows, we may have been impressed. Anyway, enough about the eating part of the Day Skipper practical course. I'm sure you get the gist.

It turned out that Nobby also had a rather archaic, military and, it could be said, spiritual style of teaching. He certainly liked to invoke Jesus Christ at regular intervals, at volume and generally in my direction. He didn't appear to have much patience when it came to imparting knowledge, or even for us to make mistakes. We suspected that the teaching part of his life was the only way he could fund what he really wanted to do, which was sail by himself. We were a bit of an inconvenience.

The best illustration of his nature and how not to be

a motivating teacher came when we were leaving Fowey after the night sail (which I'll come to in a minute). Nobby's preferred method of instructing was to stand by saying nothing, wringing his hands together with a gleeful smirk on his face until I messed up! As I approached the mouth of Fowey harbour, Nobby exploded with rage, shouting "Jesus Christ!" and other expletives, and accused me of putting all my crew in danger. All the crew in this case being him and Bob. My crimes were leaving the shelter of the harbour without first putting the sails up and motoring slightly too fast. My view of successful teaching methods involves giving you a gentle verbal prompt to guide you towards success, not to bully people into submission.

I was so taken aback by this particular outburst that I found myself trying to read the hand-held compass upside down and back to front, and became almost immobilised. I had the feeling that this was the desired effect, and that he got his thrills by reducing women to tears. Flustered I was, but tearful I wasn't. I was just plain angry. I would have left the course there and then – or rammed his boat into the nearest pile of rocks – but I decided to endure silently for the time being, vowing to make my move later. Nobby the gnome would get his just desserts, and it was going to be the gourmet option. As all this was going on, I saw Bob glance briefly up from his *Financial Times*.

Nobby and I had intermittent times of getting along reasonably well and, ultimately, I did learn quite a lot from him, even though it was education by intimidation. After all, I was the only one doing the Day Skipper syllabus, and he was all but ignoring Bob, so I had his full attention most of the time. I was concentrating so hard on my own stuff that it was a while before I noticed how little Bob was participating. I wouldn't call Bob lazy but, put it like this, if the option is reading the *FT*, having a glass of wine or listening to *Test Match Special* versus learning how to tie a bowline knot, Bob will inevitably opt for the former. He needs – what shall I call it? – encouragement.

As I had learned on the Competent Crew course, and now anticipated with a mixture of dread and thrilled anticipation, one of the Day Skipper requirements is to do a night passage. The night passage was to be done at the end of the third day. We had sailed into Noss Mayo in the afternoon, and the plan was to head back to Fowey during that night. We had an early dinner in the pub, and I watched with some trepidation as Nobby sank a couple of pints and several whiskies. Bob also had a few beers, and some! I stuck to my Diet Coke and hoped that it would all be okay in the dark with a sozzled crew. I managed to navigate my way successfully out of the Newton Ferrers estuary, and we set sail westwards into the darkening skies. I was a little concerned that Nobby and I were clipped together rather closely in the cockpit while Bob was comatose in the saloon below. Nobby was, however, surprisingly reasonable company during the night.

I was also concerned about crossing Plymouth Sound in the dark, as I imagined whole fleets of ships going back and forth out of such a busy harbour, but all we saw was one big ship on the horizon, and could easily identify that there was no danger of collision. Most of the night passage was straightforward and uneventful, which was an enormous relief.

Night navigation is all to do with light configurations. Different buoys have different light colours and sequences to guide you through a passage. Ships are a different kettle of fish as, unlike buoys, they are mostly on the move, except if moored. Each ship type has its own distinguishing set of lights. The colour and position of the lights indicates what their heading is and whether there is any likelihood of collision. To undertake a night passage safely, it's crucial to know all about lights, and this is an important part of both

Day Skipper theory and Day Skipper practical.

Most of the night passage had been uneventful until we reached Fowey at about 2.30 a.m. When we arrived at the mouth of the estuary, we couldn't see the appropriate leading lights into the harbour. Nobby started to have an all-out panic as we moved steadily towards a barely visible rocky outcrop. We needed to make a sharp turn at a particular point to avoid it, but only when we saw the special lights to starboard indicating it was time to do that. At what seemed like the last moment, the lights appeared, and we realised that they had been obscured by a huge security spotlight on the edge of a building. None of it was my fault, for once – which is always nice – and, once the bulging veins in Nobby's neck had subsided, we tied up in the harbour and crashed out in our cabins. Bob had slept through the whole experience, and he woke up later that morning wondering where he was. Ireland we said, but he didn't believe us.

The weather throughout the previous few days had been settled, and on our final day there was only a moderate pickup in the wind to suggest that it was about to change. We eventually left Fowey estuary with my sail-hoisting trauma behind me, and expected a gentle sail. However, as we tuned in to listen to the inshore waters forecast on the VHF radio, we learned that a gale was imminent. The gods had finally listened to my plea for an early end to being stuck in a confined space with a disagreeable miniature baboon. Since in boat-speak 'imminent' has a specific meaning, namely within six hours, we had to get out of harm's way as soon as possible, and sprinted directly back to base as fast as the boat could take us.

Once safely back in the harbour, it was down to me to park the boat up against the pontoon. I admit it wasn't the greatest piece of parking, as I was being blown off by the wind, and I missed it by about eighteen inches. The whole point of being on a course in the first place is to be taught how to do this properly, and if you could do it already you wouldn't be on the course. A couple of men who were standing on the pontoon kindly took our lines for us while Nobby jumped up and down shouting the usual expletives. Bob stepped off as we were pulled in, but wasn't sure how to tie us up because no one had taught him how to do it. Nobby was now "Jesus Christing" at Bob. Not a good move, I thought. I saw that Bob had turned away with his shoulders raised in an 'I'm going to take a swing at that jerk any minute' kind of way. I was torn between letting Bob let Nobby have it or being a calming influence. Still aware that I needed Nobby to sign me off as an official Day Skipper, I caught Bob's eye and made a gesture for him to stay calm for the moment.

We finished tying the boat up in silence, and I steered my unhappy husband away from Nobby, the boat, the pontoon and anything else connected with sailing. We headed for the nearest tea shop. Over tea, we decided that the certificate wasn't as important as venting our spleen, and certainly not as satisfying. We hadn't quite finished the course – there was half a day left – but were going to mutiny and jump ship early. We weren't prepared to put up with Nobby, the nauseating gnome, any longer.

When we got back to the boat, Nobby had reverted to the more jolly version of himself, and seemed just a little sheepish. "We're going home," we said. "Why?" he said. "Because you've been a complete s**t," we said. "Thanks for the feedback," he said. "I'll take it on board," he said. "Congratulations. You've both passed," he said, and we all went off together to get some fish and chips.

Flotillas, charters and the *Blue Lady*

The time had come for us to take the plunge and take a boat out on our own. If we didn't do that, we'd be destined to share boats with unpredictable people whether we went round Britain or not.

We decided to book a charter boat from Sunsail for a five-day session in the Solent, and gave Karen a call to arrange for her to come with us for three of the five days, after which we would drop her off and do the remaining two by ourselves. We thought this was a perfect way of smoothing the transition between an assisted to an unassisted passage. Starting off with Karen meant that we would have a supervised practice run out of Portsmouth, and then back in again when we dropped her off, in that way being able to check out all the potential hazards en route while still in safe hands. We marvelled at the fact that anyone was prepared to risk leaving us in charge of a yacht at all. But Karen seemed to have faith and, frankly, that's what you need when you want to make progress with a precarious activity like learning to sail at the age of fifty.

Taking a boat out on your own for the first time is tough on the nerves. When you're heeling at 30 degrees on a close reach (heading nearly straight on into the wind), it takes a while to convince yourself that the lead-weighted keel under the hull will stop the boat capsizing. Trying to manoeuvre in confined spaces feels like driving on ice, and at the back of your mind you're always aware that boats don't have brakes.

In fact, of all the boat arts, stopping and parking

your boat has to be among the most tricky. It's something that only really comes with experience, so you have to go through all the agonies of experimenting in order to get that experience. To stop, you have to slow down first, but there's the movement of the tide, the strength of the wind and the boat's momentum to consider, all of which are different every time you attempt do it. When you are experimenting, it's frequently among other yachts and motor cruisers that are worth millions of pounds. A quick getaway is out of the question on a small yacht.

Did we really want to say goodbye to Karen? Did we really want to bother sailing a boat ourselves, never mind sail around Britain? Why did we want to introduce a new source of aggravation and stress into our lives? Shouldn't we be tending our tomatoes, or taking up bridge? It was the thought of tomatoes and bridge that helped us make the decision to feel the fear and do it anyway. How bad could it be?

We reluctantly dropped Karen back in Port Solent at the end of the third day, and prepared ourselves to leave on our own the following morning. Karen had suggested that we kept it simple, and recommended that we sailed about a bit for a few hours, and then go to the Folly Inn on the Isle of Wight as our first port of call. The pontoons at the Folly are long enough to house a tanker, so it would be hard to make a total hash of the mooring. I tried practising my lassoing skills just in case. The weather was perfect, all other boats conveniently steered clear of us, and it all went like a dream. We had survived our first day of sailing all by ourselves, and celebrated in the Folly Inn that evening.

The second day was the exact opposite and we had our first (of a few!) scary sailing experiences. The weather at the Folly seemed fair and the winds gentle, but when we came out into the Solent the wind was gusting up to 30 knots. We stupidly tried to put the sails up where there was little shelter and didn't cleat them off properly, so they were flogging wildly. The boat was rocking around like a white knuckle fairground ride, and we nearly grounded ourselves on the shallow sandbanks at the mouth of the river estuary. This was all well beyond my lowly Day Skipper level, but I remembered that I was supposed to be in charge and needed to assert myself in an authoritative and sea-person-like way. I stifled a whimper, and stated that we had to turn back immediately. We hauled in the sails and limped back to Cowes marina, and spent the next few hours hugging large, frothy cappuccinos and stuffing down fruit cake in an attempt to sooth our frazzled nerves. We wondered if we'd ever be able to leave the Isle of Wight. I'd often wondered what it would be like to live there.

Karen was calm and sweet on the phone when we rang to tell her that it was far too dangerous to leave the Isle of Wight, and that we'd have to spend the night there. "Of course you can manage to sail back today," she said. "As soon as the tide turns, the sea will be smoother and the wind is going to drop. Motor along the north coast of the Isle of Wight, and then cross over to Portsmouth when you get level with Ryde. If you do that, you can stay in shelter from the south-east wind for most of the time." Sunsail needed the boat back that evening because someone else had booked it the following morning and they were worried that we were serious about not coming back.

Karen was right about everything. We did manage, and even ended up sailing across to Portsmouth because the sea was flatter and the wind had calmed down, just like she said it would. We were very relieved to tie the boat up in Port Solent after what had been a gruelling day but, miraculously, we hadn't been put off. We had a brilliant idea for our next unaccompanied sailing adventure, and it was going to be a lot less complicated: a flotilla holiday in the Mediterranean.

A flotilla is a small fleet of vessels, and what better way to spend time on a boat than in the company of other similar boats and with people of a similar level of experience. Among other exotic venues such as the Caribbean, flotillas can be found in the tideless Mediterranean, where the water is warm, the wind is gentle and sailing practice couldn't be more enjoyable. It is debatable, however, just how much sailing practice you actually get when you're island hopping, anchoring in tranquil bays, swimming off the boat, sunbathing and having extended lunches on board. The bevy of boats is looked after by a small group of experienced team leaders, and they're only a radio call away if you have any problems. They organise a variety of social activities if you want to participate, and are on hand to help you moor your boat safely at the end of the day.

Flotillas can be graded by difficulty, which is based on the navigational challenges and the level of wind you're likely to encounter. We chose level zero, as any lower than that would be a land-based holiday and wouldn't involve a boat at all. There is usually a description of the sailing area and ports of call, which acts as a clue to the type of clientele that might be on the flotilla. We avoided the one with 'lively night life', and opted for the one with 'tranquil evenings in tiny harbours and secluded coves'. It was always going to be a trade-off, because the decent showers were in the places with the night life, but we were going to take copious amounts of wet wipes with us and I would have to forgo the hairdryer for a week.

The clientele on our flotilla was mainly as you would expect, which was the type that couldn't really be bothered having to socialise with a load of other people they didn't know but would put up with it in order to have the security of being in a group. None of us had bargained for being joined by a boat load of big, tough, tattooed ex-army lads with their Eastern European girlfriends, who were only with us because they'd booked at the last minute and the flotilla with the all-night party itinerary was fully booked. Instinctively, we felt like it was a good idea to stay on good terms with this group, so we made a point of exchanging pleasantries with them and their girlfriends and struck up conversations about Greece's contribution to world history, culture and philosophy, with particular reference to Socrates and his student Plato.

As we suspected, it didn't take long before they'd managed to disrupt the status quo. They left us alone – probably due to the intellectual bond we'd managed to establish with them – and earmarked a boat load of Americans as their source of entertainment. Having come across a dead sheep's head on one of the islands, they tied it in a clear plastic bag on to the anchor chain of the American boat. When the Americans hauled the anchor up they experienced the full horror of unexpectedly coming face to face with the dead sheep's head. They clearly didn't appreciate the subtle humour of the honest British Johnny and insisted that the offending boat was expelled from our flotilla. We heard on the grapevine that the expelled boat had been allowed to join the flotilla with the lively night life after all. Well, it could have been worse; it could have been a horse's head!

Over the next two years, we went on several more flotillas and one bareboat holiday, all in Greece. The flotillas in June and early September were all very pleasant, but our bareboat trip was a last-minute cheap deal in mid-May, the weather was diabolical and the sea was freezing. We'd do better to stay in England, we thought, after battling with gales and a swell that we didn't know was possible in the Med.

So, our next step was to brave UK waters again. Going off season can be a huge financial advantage when chartering a boat, but we weren't sure how wise we were being when, at the Boat Show, we signed up to borrow a good, solid Swedish boat for half the normal rate for five days in mid-March. As March was approaching, I was regretting agreeing to this, and imagined that I was going to freeze to death as we hacked our way through ice flows. Bob accused me of exaggerating, but what did he know about feeling cold? This is the man who slept naked, half out of his sleeping bag, with the tent flap open in May in England, and couldn't sleep because he was too hot while I was curled up in a fetal ball, fully dressed with hat and gloves, and couldn't sleep because I was too cold. I dug my hot-water bottle out and bought some of the thickest thermals I could find.

If our charter boat had been a human, she would have graced the covers of *Vogue*. She had beautiful lines, was graceful and elegant and was called *Blue Lady*. We were hooked on her even before we left Port Hamble, where she was berthed. Within hours of setting off, we noticed what a difference there was between the way an average, cheaper, fibreglass flotilla boat sails and the way *Blue Lady* sailed. *Blue Lady* somehow felt more solid and dependable and, without a doubt, it was all so much easier. The weather turned out to be quite pleasant, as it does sometimes in March, and, although there was a chill in the evenings, there was a brilliant heater on the boat which warmed us up within minutes. It was so much fun, and cosy with it, and we were beginning to cope well with planning and executing small journeys around the Solent.

In fact, it was going so well that we felt brave enough to branch out a bit from the Solent and head to Poole. Being unversed in the art of navigation at that stage, Bob had a mild panic as we left the western end of the Solent in misty conditions, thought we were heading to France and wouldn't believe me when I assured him we were going directly west towards Studland. He's now a lot better at understanding how the compass works, and knows that when the compass says 270 degrees it's west and not south. After about half an hour of trying to convince him that we were definitely going to Poole, Bob realised that he'd been looking at the wrong port on the chart plotter, and conceded that I did know what I was doing and that I had been right all along. This was a pattern that had a tendency to repeat itself fairly frequently during the course of the next year or so. It was only after Bob had finally done navigation to Coastal Skipper standard that we were really able to discuss matters rationally. He finally understood the same things as I did and the reasons behind the decisions I made. I was still skipper though.

Sailing *Blue Lady* was fabulous, so we chartered her again the following June and decided to try for France, which was seriously branching out for us. The basic navigation, however, seemed straightforward. We'd read that, if you point your boat at about 180 degrees, the two opposing tides would cancel each other out and you'd land in Cherbourg. That all sounded fairly manageable, but only if the weather was mild and there hadn't been a typing error in the article. In preparation, we made our way from Port Hamble to Portland marina near Weymouth.

Portland marina was a joy to visit. There was bags of room, spacious pontoons and a funky restaurant called the Boat that Rocks, named after the movie that was filmed in the harbour. Weymouth, with its quaint old town, maritime history and long, clean beaches, was on the doorstep. When people watching from the safety of a beachside bench, we did notice that there seemed to be a bit of a problem with obesity, but perhaps it was because in Weymouth flashing the flesh was de rigueur, which made the problem more visible than, say, Cheltenham, where there aren't quite so many people wearing size 6 miniskirts and crop tops, regardless of their actual size.

It was very tempting to stay put in Portland, but France beckoned, and we could always visit again on the way back. We set the alarm for 5.30 the following morning in order to leave at first light. The journey was going to take about twelve to thirteen hours, and we wanted to arrive in daylight. It was hard to sleep properly with the prospect of crossing the English Channel ahead of us, but Bob had prepared some breakfast bacon butties in advance, which was going to make getting out of a warm bunk more attractive. Incentives on a boat usually come in the form of food, drink or a hot shower.

Throughout the night, I could hear the wind howling in the rigging of the other boats in the marina, and wondered if it was going to be too windy to go. We woke at 5.30, and could still hear what sounded like a strongish wind. We sat in silence, inwardly agonising about whether to risk going or not. After a long period of tension, we came to the same conclusion at the same time that we should go out and have a look and, if it seemed too blowy, we'd just turn back. This was a policy we've since applied many times on our journey round Britain, and it always helped reduce the angst about whether we were making right or wrong decisions if we were unsure. When we came out of the harbour entrance, the conditions proved to be perfectly acceptable. Wind whistling in the rigging can be a deceptively evil sound and can instill fear into the strongest of hearts.

Blue Lady took us to Cherbourg, and then on to Alderney in the Channel Islands. Between the Cherbourg Peninsula and Alderney there's a stretch of water called the Alderney Race. The race has some of the fastest and most dangerous currents in the world. The sea funnels south down a ten-mile-wide stretch between mainland France and Alderney, and if you get swept into it you would end up in Guernsey. We didn't want to end up in Guernsey, so we sailed in a five-mile arc round the top of where the

Alderney Race begins, just to be on the safe side. When we were safely ensconced in Alderney, we went to have a look at the race from a high point on the coast, and it looked like the sea was pouring downhill. The sheer power of the water was daunting, and we could see why you needed to treat it with respect. We headed back to Hamble, pleased with our mini adventure across the English Channel, and feeling like we had made respectable progress at last.

The various flotillas we'd been on, our bare boat holiday and chartering the *Blue Lady* had all been great experiences for us, and we were now beginning to see what kind of boat would suit us for our 'big' journey. *Blue Lady* was a Swedish-designed boat, made by the company Hallberg Rassy, and Swedish boats were apparently particularly good for negotiating difficult European waters. We were so impressed with the way she sailed, we wanted to get something similar for our trip round Britain. Our search for the right boat was on.

The Decision to Buy

If you're going to sail round Britain, having a few sailing skills is fairly important, but the most crucial thing is to be in possession of a good boat. There are many tales of people who have done the trip in the equivalent of a floating bathtub, with sails made out of old tarpaulins, nowhere to sleep and no means of communication with the outside world. Well, tosh to that! At our age, we wanted to do it with a certain amount of style, with every technical aid available, my favoured coordinating blue upholstery, a cupboard full of decent wine, a hairdryer and the prospect of being still alive at the end. Afterwards, we would still tell people about the terrible hardships we'd endured with leaking bilges, dodgy stopcocks, the unreliable compass and the half-dead albatross wedged in the rigging that had prevented us from ever turning left. (Hence, the ensuing unavoidable decision to go round clockwise).

We needed to find a way of getting our hands on a suitable boat. There were several options. We could borrow one, but we didn't know anyone who had one to lend. We could charter one, but we discovered that it was pretty near impossible to find a suitable one to charter for three solid months and, anyway, the cost of chartering was astronomical. Or, finally, we could buy one and, then, if we never wanted to set foot on a boat again at the end of the trip, we could sell it with minimum loss. We went for option three, which was to buy one and try it for size. At that stage, we had no idea how attached we would become to our boat and how selling her afterwards would be unthinkable.

Sweden apparently produced a variety of makes of good, comfortable, sturdy cruising yachts and, providing it came with a hidden drinks cabinet and the requisite level of comfort, we were definitely interested in getting one from there. With their Viking heritage, the Swedes know a thing or two about boats, particularly the sort that can easily tackle the difficult British coastline and still leave you with enough energy for a good bit of marauding and pillaging. With that in mind, we felt confident enough to bypass all the bother of doing any research on the subject and booked two flights to Gothenburg. There's an area on the west coast of Sweden just north of Gothenburg called Orust, which is famous for boatbuilding and is home to a number of builders, and this seemed like a good place to start.

We were dangerously close to being consumed by that well-known condition called 'instant gratification', after we found ourselves installed on a secondhand, 38-foot, red and white boat called a Najad. Olaf the agent had left us by ourselves with a fridge full of refreshments and plenty of bedding to spend a night on board. They're clever these Swedes! He hoped that we would 'get the feel' of the boat overnight, ready for our test sail the following morning. The boat was a fine example of superb craftsmanship, with beautifully hand-varnished teak inside and out, and cupboard doors that didn't squeak. Olaf came to take us out the following day, but there was no wind and no chance to do much more than float aimlessly on a turquoise sea in brilliant sunshine. It seemed like a perfectly adequate test to us. What else did we need to know? We did, however, manage to exercise some restraint, and asked for time to consider while we went off for a quick look round the boatyard at some of the brand new boats being manufactured by Najad.

We'd never been to a boatyard before – let alone

examined the inner workings of a boat – so the guided tour was a revelation. We saw all the different stages of manufacture, met the man that painstakingly did the ten coats of varnish by hand, and saw all the intricate details that were incorporated in the structure of a cruising yacht. No wonder they were so expensive! We'd combined the search for a boat with a few days' holiday around the archipelago, so we put the decision to buy on hold for a little while longer and went off to explore Sweden.

Sweden was, not surprisingly, full of stereotype big, blonde, strikingly healthy-looking specimens of Northern European humanity. It must be all the raw herring they eat. The Swedes seemed friendly enough in the shops and restaurants, but we were surprised by the fact that they don't make eye contact, smile or say hello when passing on a street or even on a more remote walk when you are the only other people in the vicinity. We thought the Brits were bad at that, but the Swedish are in a league of their own. It seemed fairly rude to us, but perhaps acknowledging strangers was a form of intrusion in their eyes.

We were enthralled by the west coast of Sweden. The coastline is gorgeous and studded with small islands and tiny wooden dwellings. Many of the dwellings are pretty, coloured holiday houses built right at the water's edge. The waterways around the islands make a wonderful cruising area, and life in July in Sweden is clearly outdoor heaven. The water was warm and would have been inviting but for the massive number of pink jellyfish. There were jellyfish everywhere, and the gaps between them weren't big enough to risk swimming, so we didn't.

In the towns and villages, the atmosphere was fun and buzzy but, because of the exchange rate, the cost of living for us tourists was agonisingly expensive. In one restaurant, we paid more than £40 for a bottle of Penfolds, which is only about £6 a bottle at home. It was enough to make us weep. In several restaurants we did battle with shellfish that didn't have much fish inside and the bill was what you'd expect in a Michelin-star restaurant. We ended up raiding our emergency chocolate supplies to avoid an attack of night starvation.

We hadn't realised that viewing boatyards could be so much fun, and were keen to see more. We wanted to see the Hallberg Rassy boatyard, the makers of *Blue Lady*, and their boatyard was only a few miles down the road from the Najad boatyard. The Hallberg yard was much bigger, and we were shown around several different-sized models in mid production, from a 37-footer, which would be the size we would go for, to a 60-footer, which we thought we might get in our next incarnation as round the world yachtspeople. We were now in a dilemma because we liked the Hallberg boats as much as the 38-foot Najad. I couldn't help being influenced by the fact that all Hallbergs are blue and white, which to me is a much more boaty colour, whereas the Najad was mid red with a pinky-red upholstery, which is more adobe hacienda than nautical. I felt that I should keep that opinion to myself for the moment so as not to hurt anyone's feelings and lose nautical credibility. We knew now that it was going to be a toss-up between the Najad and a second-hand Hallberg, if we could find one. The search was on and I thought blue thoughts as much as possible.

Almost as soon as we'd returned home, Bob sped off again, this time to Holland, to check out a 3-year-old Hallberg Rassy 37 he'd spied on the Internet. The blue thoughts had worked their magic. It was a perfect boat, in nautical blue, and, in the space of a few weeks, we found ourselves on the verge of owning our own boat. At that stage, we'd only vaguely addressed the issue that the boat was in Holland, and we wanted it to be in Lymington, but things do have a tendency to sort themselves out. There were a few logistics involved, but we somehow managed to get the boat and ourselves kitted out in Holland in readiness to sail it back across the English Channel. We'd already been to Cherbourg on *Blue Lady* by this stage and bummed about in the Solent a bit, but sailing from Holland to Lymington was going to be much more of a challenge, and, hopefully, we would be up to it.

Bringing *Bella Rosa* back from Holland

When we took possession of our new boat, she was called *Sterna*, and must have been named after a type of bird, or one of Iceland's leading bus companies. Whichever one it was, we didn't exactly warm to it, even if Icelandic buses were renowned for their reliability. Renaming was a must, but, after making that decision, we discovered that nautical lore has it that changing a boat's name is highly unlucky. We were going to be faced not only with the wrath of Neptune but stern disapproval from *Sterna* as well. Looking at the long list of other nautical superstitions, renaming the boat looked like it was going to be the least of our worries. When it's thought to be unlucky to allow women on board, to see a redheaded person or a flat-footed person prior to getting on board (how would you tell if someone was flat-footed?), to have black travelling bags (all of ours were black), to set sail on a Friday or to look back at the port of departure (you'd never be able to wave goodbye to anyone) and a long list of other don'ts, it makes you wonder how we ever became a successful maritime nation.

On the subject of it being unlucky to have women on board, the historical get-out clause was for the offending women to get naked and hang forwards off the bow, and that would calm the sea. I wondered if they had to sing 'My Heart Will Go On' as well. It's hard to imagine which gender thought that one up. Even though it was difficult to take many of those nautical superstitions seriously, we know of many eminent sailors who do, and we couldn't help feeling a tiny lurking sense of anxiety about changing names.

We decided that the best course of action was to stop reading about nautical superstitions, most of which came about when the general population still thought the world was flat and reaching the age of thirty was considered a good innings. They were no longer relevant, particularly the one about the black travelling bags. We decided to risk a name change and choose something more feminine and attractive that would sound good when trying to impress people, and comprehensible when sending out a May Day. It had to be a name that slipped off the tongue easily and was significant to us in some way. Some boats seem to have crazy names, with no thought to how difficult it would be to repeat them three times in a row when making radio calls. One boat we had on a Greek flotilla was called *Analysis Two*, and it was impossible say it more than twice without becoming tongue-tied and incoherent. Another boat we came across was called *Safe Arrival*, which struck me as tempting fate. Mind you, the skipper of *Safe Arrival* had, he said, survived a recent storm in the Azores, so it had worked so far.

I started to think up some useful names that might get the May Day message across more urgently like 'Help, We're Sinking', or 'Don't Panic', which reminded me of the joke about the German coastguard's response to the May Day message from a boat that said it was sinking, which was "Vot are you sinking about?" Choosing a suitable boat name was going to involve some careful consideration.

Having decided not to buy into the whole superstition thing, we thought it best to discuss our plan with *Sterna*. After all, she might have a view on the matter, and we didn't want to upset her if she was dead set on keeping her name, particularly as our safety was going to be very much in her hands. We explained that, although Sterna as a name was acceptable, she could have a pretty, more feminine, name instead, but could keep her original name in silent brackets if she wished. After ploughing through several bottles of Dutch beer, we had a strong sense that she approved of this idea and was keen to add a touch of glamour to her life and, ultimately, was happy to give it a go. We ceremonially flicked some of the beer on deck, and rechristened her *Bella Rosa* after the middle names of our two daughters. Now came the big task of getting *Bella Rosa* home.

It's two hundred and twenty-five nautical miles from the marina in Holland to the marina we'd chosen in Lymington. Our route started through the more protected inland waterways of Holland and then emerged into the North Sea at Breskens. It went south-west along the north coast of Belgium and France, crossed the English Channel and then headed along the south coast to the Solent. There were going to be many hazards to watch out for, starting with getting the boat through the first lock out of the marina. We were going to have to deal with narrow canals, more locks, other boats of all shapes and sizes, weather, wind, sandbanks, foreignness, French-speaking officials, customs procedures and, to cap it all, we were going to be crossing one of the busiest shipping lanes in the world: the English Channel. We had a boat we'd never sailed before in an area we knew nothing about, but we had a good pilot book, the right charts, had taken the appropriate courses, had a modicum of experience by now, and thought that, if we took one day at a time, we would get by.

Many of our friends thought we were crazy – and possibly wildly irresponsible – and that we would either need rescuing or would have to abandon the plan before getting very far. We would be happy enough to prove them wrong, but our principal motivation was to prove to ourselves that we could manage. This was going to be a big test of our abilities, and we would learn a huge amount just by doing it.

When we set off from the marina in Holland we knew that we were probably going to be in a permanent state of anxiety, but it was also very exciting. We were going to try to keep each leg of the journey reasonably short, so that we could get plenty of rest and spend a bit of time sightseeing as well.

The first part of the trip took us through a vast delta of inland waterways that make up much of the west coast of Holland. Some are connected to the sea, and are subject to the normal rise and fall of the tide, but there is an extensive network of canals as well, which are controlled by a large number of locks of all sizes. The locks were a bit daunting at first, but no one wants you to damage their boat, so there are plenty of offers of verbal and physical help when you tie up alongside other boats. We were happy to learn from anyone willing to proffer their expertise, and all the Dutch speak perfect English, so language was never a problem.

The canals and waterways are wide and accommodating to allow for the passage of the bigger commercial ships and barges that are so much a part of Holland's trading heritage. There were many extraordinarily quaint places dotted along the banks and many pretty Dutch towns to stop at along the way. There was an abundance of cheerful, red-roofed houses, windmills, churches, tulips and lots of cyclists to be seen along the towpaths and, because Holland is quite flat, we could see for miles across the gentle, green countryside without leaving the deck of our boat.

Within days of setting off, the weather became windy at a steady Force 6 or above and we found ourselves spending many days stuck in various small ports and unable to progress very far. We'd watch the weather carefully and, as soon as there was a lull in the wind, we grabbed the chance to move to the next port. This was how we made our way through Holland as far as Vlissingen, the last inland port before heading out into the North Sea across to Breskens in the south.

The next part of the journey was a bit daunting. The southern part of the Dutch coast, which leads down to the short coastal stretch which is Belgium and then on to northern France, is strewn with spindly fingers of sandbanks that stretch out for miles into the North Sea. Unless you sail about twenty miles offshore, it's not possible to sail directly parallel to the coast. You have to duck and dive around the sandbanks to avoid them, and it makes for a much longer and more hazardous journey. Navigating the sandbanks was going to be a bit fraught, but they were well marked with buoys, and we just needed calm weather and slight seas. With a strong swell, the sea can break over the sandbanks and it can quickly become dangerous.

In Breskens, we met a retired couple on a boat called *Wenda*. *Wenda* was a very distinctive pale turquoise blue 'Southerly' and had a keel that could lift up if you wanted to negotiate shallower waters. They were a very experienced couple, and had been round Britain twice, the last time being the previous year when Britain was beset by frequent gales. They were, quite rightly, obsessed with looking at weather forecasts, and showed us some of the best sites available on the Internet. Most ports had Internet availability, which was invaluable when it came to getting weather forecasts. *Wenda*'s favourite site was Magic Seaweed, which was geared for surfers, but worked equally well for sailors because it gave the sea state and wave heights. All the best sailors want to know how much up and down there is going to be, especially when the height of the sea bed is as variable, as it is off the north coast of France. Not to get too technical about this, but the last thing you want to do is to be going down in the trough of a wave too much when the seabed is sticking up too much, so, knowing about a predicted sea state can make all the difference to whether you decide to set sail or not.

The couple on *Wenda* were quiet and unassuming. If you met them in the street, you'd never guess that they'd done something as brave as sail round Britain. They didn't fit into our idea of a sailing stereotype at all. Proper sailors were large, with well-clipped beards, loud, commanding voices, double-breasted navy jackets and smoked a pipe. I realised that that particular image certainly left me out of the equation unless I drastically altered my appearance. Taking on a pipe sounded like an interesting idea, but I would draw the line at growing a beard. The couple on *Wenda* were small and peaceful, with ordinary clothing, an Essex twang, and neither of them had beards. They were probably thinking similar thoughts about us.

Over our next couple of years tootling around the south coast of Britain in *Bella Rosa* we constantly met unassuming, quiet people, who confessed to having undertaken some amazing journeys by yacht, but you'd never guess just by looking at them. We discovered that, although you can't always assume that everyone on a boat has masses of courage and a spirit of adventure, so many of them have, and it's misplaced to judge otherwise. There is also a category that falls into the introverted loners group, whose sole mission seems to be to avoid the rest of humanity by living on a rusty, mobile rubbish tip with a sail, and dive for cover when anyone tries to speak to them. This species often do have beards, but they are straggly and unkempt, and they usually have big holes in their navy blue Guernsey jumpers. Sailors are, without a doubt, a unique but varied species, although I'm not one to stereotype people.

We set off from Breskens feeling a little intrepid and more than a little anxious about the trials of the tricky coastline ahead. We intended to stop either in Ostend or go on to Nieuwport, depending on how the journey went. The weather, although still manageable, appeared to be closing in as we approached Ostend. *Wenda* had left before us, and we saw a boat with a distinctive turquoise hull that we judged to be *Wenda* on a course further out from us and going beyond Ostend. Nieuwport was only another ten miles, so we decided to carry on, especially as *Wenda* seemed to have decided it was okay to keep going.

By the time we reached Nieuwport the wind had become stronger and the swell was increasing. The entrance to Nieuwport was narrow and exposed, and the tide, fuelled by a north-west wind, was surging into the entrance. Some of the waves were beginning to break as they hit the side walls of the harbour entrance. We knew that we'd underestimated the risk we'd taken and that our timing was crucial in order to get through the entrance safely without being washed sideways on to one of the two pillars marking the entrance of the narrow channel. We crossed all of our fingers, held our breath, caught a moderate wave and surfed directly through the centre of the pillars. Thankfully, luck was on our side, because we made it through safely.

We realised that we had made our first conscious mistake by not quitting when conditions were still favourable. We should have gone into Ostend earlier and, even if it had been *Wenda* out there, we shouldn't have assumed that they were making a decision that would also be right for us. It turned out that the boat we saw wasn't *Wenda* after all. We bumped into them later and found out that they had ducked out in Ostend. We got away lightly with the Nieuwport incident, but it provided a big lesson in the art of making good decisions and not allowing ourselves to be wrongly influenced by others. On the positive side, it was one large step towards gaining valuable experience and an understanding that it's sometimes just plain foolhardy, not gutsy, to carry on rather than to quit and run for cover in good time.

The second scary moment came in Dunkirk, but this time we couldn't blame ourselves. We were thrilled that we'd made it that far, and began to conjure up a little of our own version of the 'Dunkirk spirit'. We chose to stay in the marina nearest to the entrance. French pontoons are generally not well known for being sturdy. They're thin and have a tendency to bounce up and down like a diving board. If, when you get off your boat to moor up, you take more than a gentle step on to the pontoon, you're likely to be jettisoned off the other side straight into the water or – even worse – another boat. It nearly caught me out, but I stopped myself just in time.

The Dunkirk marina seemed protected enough until later that evening when a malevolent Force 10 gale blew through the English Channel. The whole marina full of boats spent the night bouncing up and down like yo-yos. We were terrified that the cleats on our boat would be yanked off as the pontoon and *Bella Rosa* were battered and twisted apart and together by the strong winds. It was a very real prospect that we would end up being smashed to pieces or that another boat would break its moorings and career into us. We seemed to be the only human life in the marina, and it felt like a really bad idea being there, but we had nowhere else to take refuge. It was much too late to check into a hotel.

We were up all night checking and adjusting ropes, and made what turned out to be a very sensible decision never to go on deck alone. Bob had felt a banging and went to see how far *Bella Rosa*'s bow was off the pontoon. It was too close for comfort and we realised we needed to quickly adjust the relevant ropes before she was damaged. It was dark, raining and very windy. I insisted that Bob should wear his life jacket, and for once he didn't demur.

We waited for a lull in the wind and the surge to push *Bella Rosa* back, and each time Bob grabbed the opportunity to shorten the spring. He was bent double holding the full weight of the boat with only one turn on the cleat. I was terrified the cleat would yank off with Bob on the end of the rope and nothing to help him hold *Bella Rosa*. After five minutes or so, I saw that Bob had done as much as was possible to protect *Bella Rosa* from bashing the pontoon, and I told him to OXO off and come back on board. As is so often the case, it's at the end of tricky tasks or manoeuvres that accidents occur. Maybe you relax too much, thinking the danger has almost passed, maybe you're tired or maybe it's a bit of both these things.

Bob did his OXO and was on his knees on this narrow pontoon putting a locking turn in the rope. I was groping my way along the deck from the bow when I saw Bob's left knee slip off the pontoon with the weight of his left shoulder against the hull of *Bella Rosa*, the only thing stopping him from slipping in the water. The pontoon was rocking, the boat was moving up and down and my husband was holding on for grim death. I lunged forward, threw myself on the guardrail and grabbed the top of his life jacket just as his left leg went into the water. "Get your leg out of the water!" I yelled.

Bob sounded desperate. "I can't. I'm at a difficult angle. You've got to pull me up."

With all my strength I pulled. Bob edged his right leg further on to the pontoon. He was spreadeagled on this narrow pontoon but finally had enough purchase to get his leg out of the water. He lay face down on the pontoon. I was bent double over the guardrail not letting go until I was sure Bob was okay.

It was 3.00 a.m. by the time we'd got back on board, dried off and had a comforting cup of tea. There's no doubt that if I hadn't been able to grab him Bob would have ended up between the boat and the pontoon and who knows how serious that would have been. We still shudder to think.

We eventually crashed out with tiredness at about 4.00 a.m. as the winds began to drop. The full measure of the storm became apparent the next morning when we came on deck to find a distraught lone skipper standing by his badly damaged boat having survived being out in the channel in the full force of the gale. His boom was badly broken, his sails were ripped to shreds and, despite managing to find refuge in our marina, he ended up having his boat cleats yanked off by the force of the bounce of the pontoon. He was a wreck, his boat was a wreck, and he didn't seem very happy. I was going to point out that at least we were all still alive, but there was something about his Gallic demeanour that made me keep those thoughts to myself.

In the midst of all this, we'd received an advisory text from an experienced sailor friend saying "There's always the ferry". It was nice that someone at home was thinking about us, but we'd got this far and, in any case, we were in Dunkirk and still full of the Dunkirk Spirit. We had no intention of giving up. We were going to make it all the way home.

Our anxiety levels were still keeping us in full alert mode after more than ten days of wild winds and disconcerting experiences, and we still had to cross the busiest shipping lane in the world: the Strait of Dover. About four hundred commercial ships a day pass through this narrow channel and, what's more, it's criss-crossed by umpteen ferries from ports either side of the channel. It was a worrying prospect.

Luckily, there are strict rules of conduct when it comes to shipping lanes. One rule relevant to us was that you must cross at a right angle to give the oncoming traffic the best possible view of your boat. It can take several miles for a cargo ship to slow right down and, unlike a car, they aren't able to swerve to avoid you at the last minute. They need quite a lot of time even to change course. For these reasons, it's always prudent to pass behind them and not in front if the ship is judged to be within possible collision distance.

Small boats are also warned that the person on watch on the bridge might not be able to see you because of all the containers piled up in front of their windscreen, or that they may not have checked the radar recently. These ships are driven by mere humans after all, and there is such a thing as human error. A 37-foot yacht is a mere pimple by comparison. The thought of all these things when there is only one ship within sight isn't so bad, but when there is a whole raft of them steaming along at 20 knots to your 5, peak concentration levels are a must. We made some restorative sandwiches to keep at the ready, and put some chocolate within grabbing distance. I could see that we were going to need as much readily available sustenance as possible on this particular leg of the journey.

The day we set off from Dunkirk to Dover was the clearest and loveliest of sunny days. The visibility was such that, as we came level with Calais, we could see the white cliffs of Dover glimmering seductively in the distance. It was a magical sight for us, and our spirits rose in anticipation of finally reaching familiar shores. We turned to starboard towards the shipping lanes and scanned the skyline for oncoming ships. Extraordinarily, there seemed to be very few big ships within sight, and we only had to cross behind two ships throughout the whole stretch of the Strait of Dover. Where were the other three hundred and ninety-eight ships? It was a hallelujah moment for us as we sailed into Dover harbour and tied up our trusty *Bella Rosa* on a sturdy and reliable English pontoon on a delightfully warm and sunny day. We were beginning to feel like proper sailors and swaggered our way to the nearest quality fish and chip restaurant to celebrate our successful arrival in the UK.

We were going to do the rest of the trip in two legs. We were now in very familiar territory. After the delights of Dover, we arrived in a rough and ready Brighton. Brighton was really disappointing as a yachting destination. We had possibly the most unhelpful and indifferent welcome we've had anywhere since taking up sailing. Viewing Brighton marina from the safety of the boat, we saw what it was about just by observing the clientele. Cruisers and bruisers were in abundance, along with copious chunky gold jewellery dangling menacingly in visible chest hair. I stayed on board and Bob made a dash for the nearest shop to get fresh food supplies. When he got back, he said that I'd made a wise decision to stay put as it was a jungle out there. We had dinner on the boat and, now that the weather had improved dramatically, were looking forward to leaving for Lymington the next day – and not a day too soon.

Our final leg of the journey was to take *Bella Rosa* to her new home in Berthon marina in Lymington. Berthon was the first yacht marina to be created in Britain, and one of the most appealing things about it was that the staff were allowed to bring their dogs to work! The dogs were frequently to be seen strolling about the boatyard like true sea dogs. Berthon had originally started out as a traditional boatbuilding yard, and they'd kept that side of things going after they'd built the marina. This was a particularly attractive feature to us as we had every intention of doing as little boat maintenance as possible ourselves. We'd gladly leave the removal of stubborn barnacles and scrubbing bottoms to someone else.

We'd taken sixteen rather fraught days to sail *Bella Rosa* safely back to England but, within that time, we'd accumulated so much more sailing experience, and our confidence was steadily growing. It was mid September, and our aim now was to get as much practice as possible to prepare for the following spring. Lymington was a delightful home for *Bella Rosa*, and the Solent was right on our doorstep waiting to be explored more fully.

Getting to Know Our New Boat and Getting some Practice

After arriving back from Holland in September 2010, there wasn't much time left that first summer to get the kind of experience we were going to need if we were still planning on going round Britain in spring 2011. Late autumn and winter isn't that pleasant a time to sail, and *Bella Rosa* was going to be out of the water between the beginning of November and the following March. We were still able to sail in September and October that year, so we carried on practising around the Solent area. We had good days when we thought we knew what we were doing, and some bad days when we felt like a couple of silly old fossils who were deluding themselves thinking they could sail. During this period of getting to know our lovely new boat, we never consciously made any life-threatening mistakes, managed to keep the boat the right way up and – most importantly – whatever happened, we never ever went off the idea of sailing round Britain.

But, come the end of the season we decided that we needed more experience and time to get to know our new boat, and made the momentous decision to postpone the trip until 2012. In retrospect, it was a good decision. We might well have got round in one piece with our existing knowledge, but we would have been a lot less confident, would have had many more fraught moments and wouldn't have enjoyed the experience so much. In that extra summer of sailing, we took huge strides forwards with our confidence and experience, and had loads of fun.

As well as lots of shorter local trips, we spent four weeks in June sailing along the south coast of England to the Isles of Scilly and back and, as a consequence, became much more familiar with the different sea states and weather. The Isles of Scilly expedition was a testing run for many reasons, not least to see how we felt about being on the boat for a prolonged period. We discovered that we thoroughly enjoyed living on the boat and were reluctant to get off at the end of the four weeks.

The extra time also gave me a chance to take the Yacht Master Coastal Skipper practical course with Alex (the same amiable Alex who subsequently joined us at Newlyn as an extra hand to cross the Bristol Channel). I'd already taken the Yacht Master Coastal theory course the previous year. The weather was pretty foul during the course, and we frequently had to be out in a Force 8, but it enabled us to get plenty of experience dealing with bad conditions with an expert on board.

Alex taught us one of the most useful things of all, and that was to have confidence in our boat. He demonstrated that our boat was built for sailing. If there were going to be limits they would be ours: our preparedness and ability to be out in difficult conditions. *Bella Rosa* would handle it. More experienced sailors know this but for us it was a revelation and changed the way we approached many situations. Keeping warm, fit and well fed was the Number 1 rule! I envisaged telling *Bella Rosa* our route and letting her get on with it while I worked my way through my pile of buy one get one half price novels. I didn't want her thinking she was skipper though. That was still to be my job!

Preparation

At last, April 2012 arrived, and with it our planned date of departure round Britain. In the final few days prior to casting off, I thought that it might be prudent to give a quick nod to the appropriate sea god. Not that I'm superstitious or anything. Apparently, even some of the mightiest salty seafarers are prone to this sort of behaviour, so maybe Neptune wasn't a fictitious character after all. The strangest things have happened at sea, and it seemed to me that it was a reckless person that was prepared to trifle with such matters. There would be sufficient risks without upsetting a notoriously irascible, not to say, territorial, despot that had total control of the vast ocean that we were going to be floating about in for the next three months.

While researching the best way to go about appeasing the right gods, I became sidetracked by the list of runners in the forthcoming Grand National and, as luck would have it, I discovered that the hand of fate had gently steered me in the direction of an attractive solution that would also incorporate a bit of a flutter. The fact that there were several horses with nautical names could only be portentous. Spookily, two of them were called Neptune 'something or other', and one was called Seabass, which I felt was relevant enough, given that it was a type of sea fish.

To be sure that I wasn't missing anything more obvious, I also checked to see if there was a horse called 'Trouble-Free Trip Round Britain In Three Glorious Months of Unbroken Sunshine', but, as there wasn't, I resorted to backing Neptune Equester each way at 100 to 1 and Seabass each way at 18 to 1. Typically, I ended up backing the wrong Neptune, but it wasn't all bad. Happily, I was quids in with Seabass coming in at a respectable third. My Neptune also managed to complete the course, so that was a perfectly satisfactory result as far as I was concerned. The winnings naturally had to go towards a bottle of champagne, which we would share with Neptune (the sea god, not the horse) at a later date. We hoped that the gesture would put him in a good enough mood to keep our own small area of sea nice and calm for the next few months!

Having ticked off 'Pandering to the powers that be' on the to do list, we needed to get on with some other important jobs, such as stocking up on food and drink. We weren't about to do a prolonged Atlantic crossing, at least not intentionally, but it was still a good idea to have a decent-sized store of non-perishable food essentials, such as cans of Marks & Spencer's chicken curry, cans of soup, dried pasta, boil-in-the-bag rice, Green and Black's 85% chocolate, posh crisps, decent wine and stuff that would keep us going should we get stuck on anchor in some out-of-the-way cove for longer periods than expected. The coastline of Britain, with its tiny convenience shops, Co-ops and Spars was never going to be very far away, so we weren't going to starve to death unless we accidentally turned left instead of right when reaching Land's End or any other significant corners. I decided to make 'If in doubt, turn right' my mantra for the journey.

We considered the idea of trying to catch fish but, although it sounded like a wonderfully romantic idea in terms of being self-sufficient, I knew it was likely to be a bit hit and miss, especially with Bob at the end of the fishing rod. It wasn't something that we were going to be able to rely on if we did start to get a bit low on cans of Heinz beans, but Bob was in possession of a sea fishing rod – it was coming anyway – and it was always an option worth trying if we became desperate. Failing that, there was always the May Day procedure, but I strongly suspected that the RNLI might not be too pleased to receive an emergency radio order for a couple of deep-pan pizzas if we weren't also in grave and imminent danger.

Having the right food available is very important on a boat. You need to be well fed when you're out all day working hard in the cold and the rain but, as well as having many necessary meals on board *Bella Rosa*, we were also looking forward to eating our way round the most interesting of Britain's cafés and restaurants. We couldn't think of a better way to investigate what the different areas of Britain had to offer than eating locally-sourced food. We had a few places in mind even before we set off. We'd watched the *Coast* episode on television about Arbroath on the east coast of Scotland, and it looked like it was going to be worth the hundreds of miles to get there in order to sample an Arbroath Smokie straight from the smoker. Whitby was also famous for having the best fish and chip shop in the whole of Britain. Those two snippets of information were quite a spur, but so was the thought that there were going to be many other great eateries to try before we were anywhere near Arbroath or Whitby.

Along with filling the store cupboard, we needed to think hard about what clothes to take. When embarking upon a three-month sailing trip around the 'weather sensitive' shores of Great Britain, you know that you are definitely going to need some of that robust-looking sailing gear that you mainly find in the offshore department of a chandlery or at the Boat Show. We already had our matching waterproof salopettes and bright red jackets from Henri Lloyd. The brand name alone made us feel a little continental. We'd also bought some half-price, non-slip waterproof boots at the Boat Show the previous year. After testing them out, we suspected that they were half price because they were only half non-slip and half waterproof. However, our Henri Lloyd gear was graded for coastal offshore sailing, which just about covered everything we thought we would be likely to be doing.

The prospect of having to pack clothes to last us for three months was a bit daunting. We had to be prepared for the full range of British weather, which, as we all know, can be quite extensive and can occur at any time and sometimes all at the same time. That could include anything from snow, ice, sleet, hail, driving cold rain, driving warm rain, warm drizzle, fierce gales, gentle breezes, thunderstorms, general mugginess, sunshine and the occasional unexpected heatwave. Added to that was the fact that the boat wardrobe was only the size of a small fridge, so we had to be ruthless. If an article of clothing didn't contain jersey or Lycra and couldn't be crushed into the corner without getting wrinkly, it wasn't going to be coming. However, I did feel that, in the lofty position of skipper, it was important to keep my standards up, so I went out to buy a variety of nautically-striped tops that would indicate my status as skipper to anyone with half a nautical brain. Looking convincing in the male-dominated world of sailing is essential for the female morale. On the premise that the weather might turn out to be 50% cold and wet and 50% warm and dry, half of what we both took was thick and woolly and the other half was lightweight and cool. In the end, it was quite a while before the second category saw the light of day.

Bob was predictably oblivious to his forthcoming wardrobe needs right up to the point of departure. He swiftly shunned my suggestion that he should buy a few of those high-tech, quick-dry outfits, and stated categorically that he was going to stick to his tried and trusty collection of sport-specific-slogan T-shirts and wide range of baggy shorts. It did occur to me that washing and drying all that stuff might be a bit of a logistics problem, but a happy and comfortable crew was more important. In fact, I needed to remind myself that the whole point of having a crew was to get them to do all the dogsbody stuff like washing, drying, and especially scrubbing, in order to free up one's own time to direct operations.

In normal life, Bob wore shorts continually throughout the year, only occasionally making the transition to long trousers on 'super smart' occasions or when the weather was really severe. With that in mind, I decided that Bob's shorts-wearing habit could be useful as an additional weather gauge. If he wasn't wearing them and had trousers on instead, it would mean that it was genuinely freezing and therefore it would justify drinking copious amounts of hot chocolate and eating giant-sized sandwiches even when it wasn't lunchtime.

On the subject of T-shirts, I was worried that Bob might get confused about which particular leisure pursuit he was undertaking if the T-shirt of the day was giving him the wrong prompt. If he wasn't concentrating properly or was a smidgen tired after a long day, he might be in danger of lunging for a tennis-style drop shot in the middle of a tricky marina manoeuvre while wearing a T-shirt bearing the slogan 'How Green Was My Volley'. The possible consequences of wearing his 'Great Tackle' T-shirt in a busy shipping lane didn't bear thinking about. As a safety measure, I bought him a couple of proper sailing T-shirts with yacht motifs on them, and hoped that they would stand him in good stead during the times when things got a bit fraught. He could refer to them at any time and, indeed, so could I. The next shopping item was to be port and starboard socks.

As it turned out, we frequently piled on a third of our winter clothing supplies at any one time. We ended up wearing endless layers of thermals, fleeces, thick waterproofs, woolly hats and gloves throughout most of the trip. We could have been on an Arctic expedition. We sometimes wore so many layers that our steering ability was severely impaired. The good news was that all the marinas had industrial-sized washing machines with matching dryers, and we never had to wait to use them because hardly anyone else was mad enough to be travelling round the coast of Britain during one of the coldest summers we've experienced.

You only need one trip to Boots to get everything you need in the medical and cosmetic line – as they sell everything – but it can take hours to get round the whole shop deciding what to buy. I'd only been in there for about ten minutes when I realised that I'd already manage to accumulate the equivalent of a hypochondriac's starter kit. I hadn't realised how many conditions existed that necessitated some sort of unction or syrup to alleviate them. After reminding myself that most of these conditions were unlikely to be brought on by being on board a yacht in UK waters, I retraced my steps and put most of the stuff back, including the haemorrhoid cream and various anti-fungals. Three hours later, being on the verge of a severe migraine even though I'd never had one before, I grabbed a box of Paracetamol and a jar of 'age defying moisturising cream' and made for the checkout. If I could come back looking younger than I did when I'd set off, was I bothered about flatulence, piles or deep vein thrombosis? I don't think so!

Having organised the essentials, we turned our minds to on-board entertainment, but suspected that we would be kept pretty busy exploring new destinations and discussing the contrasts inherent in our great British culture. Much of our three months would be spent sailing, passage planning, cooking, shopping for the cooking, and generally enjoying our time as tourists looking around all those new places.

We wanted to discover the essence of those parts of Britain we knew little about, and we wanted to see if there were any discernible differences between the north, south, east and west. There was going to be some interesting and varied cultural history to discover, and we hoped to find a thriving musical tradition, especially in Ireland and Scotland. We wanted to see how the tiny communities in the remoter parts of Britain lived, and compare all the different communities we came across, from small rural areas to large industrial towns.

For those times when we wanted just to relax on board, we included a small selection of novels, a quiz book and, of course, the guitar for Bob. The guitar didn't have a lot to offer in terms of being useful around the boat and being largely unqualified as a viable crew member, but Bob could produce quite a nice sound from it, and the idea of having soothing live music on board from time to time was quite comforting. The guitar was to be allocated the fore cabin unless we ever had overnight guests, when it would have to share Bob's bunk! If there was any insubordination, or if it got any ideas above its station, I would just shout "Firewood!" very loudly.

We were also both taking our iPads, which had many fun uses as well as practical uses as an extra navigational aid and a source of weather information. Personally, I'd been inspired by David Hockney's iPad paintings, which he made using the Brushes app, and planned to have a go at doing some myself. This was likely to be one of those bad weather occupations, and I suspected most of them would be entitled 'Boat Interior'. We had a radio on board but, if we were still short of things to do, there was always the hefty and trusty *Reeds Almanac* to read through with its section on nautical terms in at least four other European languages. One day, we might well need to know what 'fender' was in Spanish.

Off at Last to Portland

We were heading off into a proverbial 'blazing sunset' and it felt quite normal, except it wasn't exactly sunset: it was 9.00 a.m. in the morning on an English Monday in the middle of April. There were clear skies, cool, crisp air and watery sunshine. We had closed the door on all regular domestic concerns the previous day, and were looking forward to three months of edited living and a chance to view the coastline of our island home from the more distant perspective of the sea. When we weren't taking refuge in a sheltered cove or friendly marina, much of the time would be spent being outside looking in. It was the year of the Queen's Diamond Jubilee, and Britain was going to be hosting the Olympic Games later in the summer, and we were sailing round it all. It felt like a truly auspicious time to be doing this trip.

We'd said our temporary goodbyes to our two daughters, Sophie and Gracie, our golden retriever, Bonnie, and to our friends at home. My parents, who lived near Lymington, came down on to the pontoon to wave us off and would be back on the same pontoon in three months' time welcoming us back again if all went according to plan. They were probably a little bit afraid for us, not being sailors themselves, but we assured them that what we were about to do wasn't dangerous, and that we wouldn't be going anywhere near the notorious whirlpool in the Gulf of Corryvreckan. That was what you could call a 'Pinocchio moment'. I hoped that they would stop watching *Coast* for the duration.

After the requisite photo session on and off the deck wearing our 'Bella Rosa Round Britain 2012' caps given to us by our friends, Sue and Richard, we finally cast off, chugged out of our marina mooring and into the full flow of the Lymington River. Within no time, we were waving our last goodbyes and were turning purposefully right towards the Needles Channel and our first destination: Portland marina.

The conditions on our first day were perfect. We were swept nicely through the Needles Channel by a strong fair tide, which just happened to be heading to Portland as well, and, although there was little wind to start with, once we passed St Albans Head we were able to switch the engine off and sail gracefully the rest of the way. The route to Portland was familiar territory to us. We'd done much of our sailing practice in the area west of the Solent and had spent many family summer holidays camping near Swanage and having picnics on the delightful National Trust-owned Studland beach. As we passed close to Studland with its protected anchorage north of Old Harry Rocks, I recalled the numerous times that I'd rented a kayak from the beach and rowed out to look more closely at the collection of yachts moored in the bay. For many years prior to taking up sailing, I'd yearned to be on a yacht anchored in Studland Bay, and we'd finally managed to do it when we were on one of our practice sailing sessions. Sitting on our own deck in the shadow of Old Harry Rocks in one of the prettiest bays on the south coast of England was every bit as tremendous as it had looked.

We continued steadily towards Portland, still feeling like it was the most natural thing in the world to be doing what we were doing, but five years earlier it would have been unthinkable. We had wondered whether we might feel apprehensive, strange or even emotional, but we felt completely at peace, as if we were popping across the

Solent for a swift drink in Yarmouth, an overnight stay in the marina, and back the following day in time for tea. Six years earlier, 'normal' for us would have been being very firmly on land, sitting on a bench on Lymington Quay, staring at the yachts moored on the town pontoon and wistfully imagining what it might feel like to be sailing out on one. Sometimes, when visiting Lymington Quay, we were compelled to sign up for the hour-long Solent sightseeing trip just to get a chance to be out on the water.

So, on 16 April 2012, it felt perfectly right and normal to be leaving the Lymington River on *Bella Rosa*, our 37-foot Swedish yacht, to embark upon a three-month trip that would take us round much of mainland Britain via the Irish Sea. Of course, we were well aware that the British coastline had a reputation for being a bit 'tricky', and that it was possible that our expedition might throw up all manner of daunting experiences – especially to relatively novice sailors like ourselves – but we felt that we'd prepared ourselves well enough and were at peace with the prospect, at least for the time being.

The idea to embark on such an expedition from the moment it had been conceived several years earlier had seemed like the right thing to do. It felt like an appropriate use of time, and didn't appear to need detailed analysis, although we knew it would necessitate a lot of hard training if we were to stay afloat and return home triumphant.

The main driving force behind our adventure was the desire to see much more of our own country. We'd spent years travelling abroad with the family for holidays, and yet there were whole swathes of Britain that we'd never visited, and whole stretches of wonderful coastline that we'd never seen. In the past, and prior to learning to sail, we'd contemplated the idea of driving round the coast, but so much time in a car would have been like watching the British land - and seascape on TV, through a glass windscreen in-between sightseeing stops. There was romance and adventure attached to the idea of travelling by boat, and the thought of doing it 'a deux' and being completely in charge of our own boat was thrilling. Choosing to go by boat rather than car might seem like total madness when considering the physical hard work involved, the wide-ranging skills needed and the strong nerve required, but, on the plus side, it would keep us away from busy motorways and allow us to commune with nature in close proximity.

This desire to sail round Britain manifested itself at a time when life's responsibilities were at a manageable minimum. Bob was a semi-retired businessman and able to be very flexible with his time, our two daughters had fled the nest and might not even notice that we'd disappeared for three months, my parents still had each other and were still very capable and independent, and my small efforts at teaching yoga and running the odd art workshop could be put on hold indefinitely. Gone were the days of thinking that taking 'gap years' and 'travelling' were for layabouts and ne'er-do-wells. We had done 'our bit' and could now guiltlessly release ourselves into a world of extended 'me time' (or, as in our case, 'us time') and do what we liked with impunity.

We were driven harder by the knowledge that this was our 'window'. It was without a doubt now or never, and we were almost possessed in our determination to see it through. This feeling of being 'driven' right from the moment I'd felt compelled to ring Sunsail did make me wonder whether I was really being used as a human channel by any number of dead sailors who couldn't kick the sailing habit even from the grave. If that was the case, I hoped I was channelling someone highly experienced like Chay Blythe and not Captain Calamity. We were open to any support and useful contributory help and advice – spiritual or otherwise – and, anyway, it all felt so exciting.

The dog had gone to live with a friend, the bills were on direct debit, the pot plants were dead already, the post was to be gathered by our helpful friends and neighbours, and our domestic life was 100% ready to be left to fend for itself. We could sail away trouble free, and needed to get on and do it before it was too late.

Sailing into Portland marina was a piece of cake, and not just because Bob was on the helm and I wasn't. The main harbour is well protected and very large, and the marina, which is situated in the far corner, has generously long pontoons with plenty of space between them. It would be difficult to make a mess of mooring the boat. Portland Harbour used to be a naval base from the 1800s, when they built the long breakwaters to keep out first the French and then the Germans. Now that we're all big mates with the rest of Europe, it's only the numerous learner dinghy sailors that pose a threat, although I did spot some very suspicious characters lurking around the motor cruisers. Some of them could easily have been foreigners.

When the navy left, the marina was built and the area became designated as an official Olympic venue for water sports. Apparently, it was the first Olympic venue to be finished, but we could see little evidence that anything had changed since our first visit three years previously. I don't know what we were expecting. Perhaps a large dome of some sort or even a Ferris wheel? Plymouth has a Ferris wheel. We were told that the Queen owns half the seabed under the pontoons, which is a very odd concept. We wondered if she came down to do a bit of crabbing when they were running a bit low on pheasants at Balmoral.

The shipping forecast had predicted gale force winds for the following couple of days, so we prepared to tuck up in the marina for at least two nights. We had told everyone we were going round Britain, but did we ever say it was going to be by boat?

We found that we liked Portland marina a lot, which was lucky because we ended up staying there for several days. The wind was blowing very hard and the sea state in Lyme Bay was rough. We decided to go for a long walk round Portland and found ourselves circumnavigating the prison, which takes up a huge area. To quote a line from a well-known 70's song, "There were plants and birds and rocks and things" with emphasis on the rocks because Portland is, of course, well known for its stone. In fact, Portland should have celebrity status, it's stone having been used to build Buckingham Palace, St Paul's Cathedral and the United Nations headquarters in New York. We had been hoping to find a nice gastropub for lunch but were forced to buy sandwiches from the Co-op instead. The locals probably didn't eat out very often due to the fact that many of them were behind bars in the famous prison.

Looking out to sea, we could see the extreme foaming white turbulence of the notorious Portland Race. Legend has it that substantial vessels have disappeared without trace in the race, and seeing it at its full Force 8 glory was a reminder of why it is crucial to give it a wide berth of several miles. There is an inner passage, but it's only really viable in calm weather, only safe to go within a very short tidal window, and we were told that there are numerous lobster pots lining the route, lying in readiness to wrap themselves round your propeller. Going via the A35 through Dorchester suddenly seemed like a great idea.

We'd arrived in Portland on the Monday, but couldn't see ourselves leaving until the Thursday or Friday. Even when the wind died down, we were acutely aware that it can still take quite a while for the sea state to calm down after the storm, and that was another serious consideration. We had to be careful that impatience didn't prompt us to set off too soon, but we had still only completed one day of our three-month expedition and were getting restless to make a move.

Portland to Dartmouth in the Rough

The day we decided to leave Portland was preceded by a night of being half awake, listening out for the winds to die down. We got up at seven o'clock, checked the latest forecast for any positive changes, and saw that the Force 8 had at least diminished to a Force 6 but was unlikely to alter further over the next few days. We consulted Coast Watch, those under-appreciated and invaluable volunteer guardians of sailing vessels that attempt to circumnavigate tricky headlands. From their Nissen hut tucked into the cliffs at the southern end of Portland Bill, they reported that the sea was still a bit rough around the Bill area. We had adopted a policy of, if we were in two minds about whether to stay or whether to go, we could always sail out to have a look and turn back if we didn't like the look of it. *Bella Rosa*, the Wonder Boat, agreed to give it a go, so that was that. To Dartmouth and beyond ...

Coast Watch had been right about the sea around the Bill being rough, even though we gave the tip of it a full six-mile radius. We still thought that it would be manageable, despite having the prospect of nine hours of being tossed around with wind against tide for the majority of the time. It was just going to be quite physically demanding. In my case, I felt seasick for the first time ever and, when I wasn't keeping the hourly log or paying an occasional visit to the heads, I was staring fixedly at the horizon trying to think of nothing. In Bob's case, he was helming for the best part of the time, and had to keep his concentration up while being regularly soaked by a face full of water when the bow hit the waves quite hard.

I discovered that feeling sick has its advantages. It might have been dangerous and scary out there, but I wasn't remotely bothered, as I was only interested in how soon the nausea would stop and how soon we would arrive in Dartmouth. I made a mental note never to agree to sail anywhere that took much longer than twenty-four hours to reach.

Despite feeling lousy, log keeping was always an essential part of each passage, and a legal requirement, so I needed to do it regardless of how I felt. Unfortunately, keeping the log up to date and trips to the heads both involved a trip down below, and every foray was seriously hindered by the large amount of Velcro on my coastal, offshore, foul-weather gear getting itself attached to things. Not being satisfied with its job of acting as a clothing fastener, it fixed itself to as much as possible en route through the saloon, including one of our blue and white striped, nautical-themed deck cushions, the Union Jack tea towel and even itself. I had never had this problem before, but we were on a roller coaster ride, and every little move I made was followed by being slammed hard against a nearby surface as *Bella Rosa* rocked her way west towards Dartmouth. If there was something soft and material-like between me and any surface, it got instantly Velcroed. The discovery of the day was that Velcro is impressively strong stuff.

To say that we were relieved finally to arrive in Dartmouth is an understatement. My sickness, along with the sea state, had finally subsided a couple of hours before we arrived. We were in a happy mood as we approached the upmarket Dart marina, and pleased to see lots of vacant spaces along their pontoons. We chose Dart marina because they advertised great facilities, like having a proper bath, a swimming pool, sauna and jacuzzi. Bob went off to have a shower and I immersed myself in a deep bath of hot water to try to thaw out. Being able to have a bath is one of the things I missed most about being on a boat, so to find one in Dartmouth was perfect compensation for our arduous day out on the ocean. We decided that the next day would be a day off to enjoy whatever the seafaring town of Dartmouth had to offer.

Dartmouth

The deep water port of Dartmouth is a bustling, working town that has seafaring connections that date right back to the Crusades, the Pilgrim Fathers and many more significant historical events. The estuary buzzes with waterborne activity and there are numerous old and historic buildings still in existence around the waterfront area. The wonky stretch of Tudor-looking shops of the Butterwalk that I originally thought were just a modern copy are completely genuine and date back to 1635. Dartmouth is steeped in the atmosphere of bygone nauticalness and is utterly charming.

In the very modern Dart marina we were moored just outside a holiday flat belonging to some friends of ours from Bath, and were considering breaking in to get a comfortable, non - rocking and rolling bed for the night. The pirate mentality was setting in strongly, but we chickened out in the end as we didn't want to risk getting banged up for breaking and entering after merely a week at sea. That night, we collapsed exhausted into our boat bunks, but the following morning woke up to a day that finally resembled summer. The previous day had been one of sheer endurance and no pleasure, and Bob had confessed to some doubts about the idea of going all the way round Britain, but our faith in the enterprise had been restored once we'd woken up to pure sunshine.

It was tempting for me to spend the whole day in the marina bath, but just for a change we decided to go on a boat trip. This time, it was a ferry trip to the Agatha Christie house further down the river. The house was bought in 1938 as Christie's summer residence, is situated in an enviable position overlooking the Dart and has extensive gardens that tumble right down to the water's edge. My overall impression was one of disappointment at the drab and uninspiring rooms and the general shabbiness of the interior. To me, there was nothing that made it stand out as belonging to a prolific literary giant. It was like some ordinary person's home. Call me a philistine but, if it was mine, I would have gutted the whole place and gone for a more bohemian, intellectual theme.

The house is now owned by the National Trust, who obviously want to keep it in the same state as when it was owned by Agatha Christie, but it could do with some restoration, and it would have been good to have more information about her life and her writing. Not wanting to criticise the National Trust too much, as they clearly do a sterling job in preserving our heritage, they can, however, always be relied upon to produce a good scone. We sought out the Old Stable café to find one, and then wended our way back to *Bella Rosa* for a lie down before tackling a cracking fish dinner at Rockfish by the waterside. Being a tourist is tough work!

Dartmouth to Plymouth

Happily, the pleasant weather continued and we left Dartmouth in a gentle breeze on a lovely sunny day. *Bella Rosa* is equipped with an amazing technical device called AIS, which shows on the chart plotter screen exactly where any nearby commercial boats are, how fast they're travelling and what course they're on. They would also be able to see our position on their screens, which is even better as it lessens the chance of being run over. En route to Plymouth, I could see on the AIS that there was a very large cargo ship belting straight for us on collision course, even before we were able to see it with our own eyes. Knowing what's out there before you can actually see it can be a mixed blessing, as it enables you to start panicking well before you otherwise would have done without the AIS. By the time the ship finally appeared on the horizon it had changed course and was going to clear us by miles. Phew!

Despite the optimistic start, the forecasts predicted much stronger, gusty winds later that day. People might think that because we were *sailing* round Britain, we would be wanting wind, but what we wanted was consistent wind at a steady, manageable, predictable rate and not the temperamental type that can't decide on a specific strength and throws intermittent big gusts around willy-nilly.

The passage to Plymouth became another session of wave bashing, enough to make the teeth rattle in our heads as we crashed along through turbulent water. We had whacking great gusts, wind against tide and there was much swearing from the Admirable Bob. Although this time I escaped the seasickness, we both felt exhausted again when we arrived in Plymouth yacht haven. We didn't leave the marina at all during our short stay, so, apart from seeing Plymouth and the surrounding area from the sea – which did look very jolly with its Ferris wheel – we missed out on any local cultural experience. We needed to crack on to get to Newlyn in time to meet our expert sailing friend, Alex, who was going to accompany us during our overnight sail across the Bristol Channel to Milford Haven. Newlyn, a small Cornish seaside town tucked into the western corner of Mount's Bay, was going to be our last port of call before rounding Land's End.

We wanted (and needed) some additional help for our night passage across to Milford Haven as we'd never done a night sail by ourselves before, and the Bristol Channel was not the place to cut our teeth. It was very reassuring to think that Alex would be with us as we rounded the rocky and frequently treacherous Land's End, and launched ourselves into the untamed waters of the Atlantic Sea. We planned to leave for Fowey early the following morning and Newlyn would be our next stop after that.

Plymouth to Fowey

Cooking on board turned out to be surprisingly easy, mainly because the Admirable ended up doing most of it. We'd invested in something called a 'Remoska', a small cooker from the Czech Republic that looks like an upside down electric frying pan on top of a metal casserole dish. It works on shore power, which is always available in marinas, and therefore saves heavily on gas. It only needs a small surface to sit on, and a nearby plug socket, and has only one switch, which is either on or off. Simple!

Everything in the Remoska takes just over one hour. You can sling in a load of chunky veg to roast with a drizzle of olive oil and pop a couple of chicken breasts on top. You can even bake scones or crumble in it, but we decided we'd pass on the baking option, as waving a bag of flour around in our confined living space would be asking for trouble. At that stage, we'd eaten 'Remoska style' five times out of six. The other meal was the fish dinner in Dartmouth. I wondered how else it could be useful. Drying small amounts of washing might work, but washing clothes was an event to be avoided for as long as possible.

We set off for Fowey with the intention of arriving by lunchtime and having a relaxing afternoon for once. There were yet more choppy seas, more gusty winds and yet another 'bucking bronco' ride, but at least it was only for four hours this time, so we were in much better spirits. We were looking forward to gentle breezes and pleasant sailing at some point in the future but, given that it was still only April, we wondered how long we would have to wait for the conditions to improve. If it wasn't for our gutsy and intrepid boat, *Bella Rosa*, we might still be in Portland now, but we were making good progress. We were feeling very optimistic that we would be in Newlyn in good time to meet Alex even if we took a rest day off in Fowey. Fowey is such a pretty place and, being April, there were very few tourists around and the harbour was awash with available visitor moorings. It was a good time to be there.

Fowey

Taking a day off in Fowey had become a necessity because a Force 8 was heading our way with great speed. *Bella Rosa* was secure on a nice large mooring buoy in the middle of the estuary, so we hailed a water taxi to take us to the town quay. We decided that we needed to get the use of our legs back, so we took an additional ferry over to Bodinnick to enable us to do a four-mile circular walk along the other side of the estuary along to Polruan and then back by foot ferry to Fowey. Despite apparently not being able to stay off boats even on our days off, our legs did for once get a bit of a look-in and seemed still to be working quite well on the flat. The hills, however, were more of a challenge. On our return to Fowey, we popped into a pub called the Lugger for a crab sandwich. It was a seafaring-themed pub and somehow they'd managed to create an effect where the whole pub felt like it was rocking from side to side like a boat. We wondered how they'd managed to get that effect. In fact, in retrospect, the whole of Fowey and its surrounding areas seemed to be rocking. Extraordinary!

Newlyn

We were becoming used to looking for something called 'weather windows', or in other words, short gaps of good weather between the bad weather where we could whizz out as quickly as possible and get to our next destination before the next bad bit of weather set in. It was like dodging bullets. Time was pressing and we spotted a weather window that would get us from Fowey to Newlyn in one hop, although it was going to be a bit more than just a hop because the journey was going to take seven and a half hours. Another Force 8 gale was forecast for 'later', which in nautical speak means more than twelve hours from the time of the broadcast. Until then, conditions were relatively acceptable, so we set sail hoping that we would be tucked up in Newlyn well before the gale blew in.

Between Fowey and Newlyn is a large promontory called the Lizard, where, like Portland Bill, the tides can become confused, difficult and sometimes dangerous. To be on the safe side, we gave it a three-mile radius, and even out there encountered some biggish rolling waves. It wasn't a problem though as there was a lot of space between them, so we just rolled pleasantly up and down keeping our teeth intact for once.

When we got to St Mount's Bay, the sea really flattened out and we had a very enjoyable three-hour sail towards Newlyn. Our arrival in Newlyn would signify the end of the beginning. From Newlyn onwards was entirely new territory: we'd be heading north and our journey round Britain was about to become a serious undertaking.

Newlyn is a proper fishing harbour and has limited places on its pontoons for visiting yachts. Being April, we were almost the only leisure sailors in evidence and easily found ourselves a comfortable berth in which to sit out the next couple of days of gales. It was very exciting to have reached Newlyn on schedule and be a perky little yacht among a haven of trawlers. This was our first 'serious' destination, as opposed to a mere 'tourist' destination, and, from here onwards, we were going to be entering unknown waters.

Exploring Newlyn

We had a full day to explore Newlyn before Alex was due to arrive later that day. Under its plain and utilitarian facade, Newlyn turned out to be quite an arty place. The proximity to St Ives and the Tate Gallery might have been influential, but the luminous Cornish light was always a draw to artists and it was easy to see the attraction. We walked along the seafront to Penzance and stopped in a lovely little gallery along the way for coffee and a bit of culture. The storm must have been pretty bad the previous night because the promenade was strewn with seaweed and pebbles. The sea was still throwing up big spray as it hit the sea wall and we had to dodge a soaking many times.

Penzance has a large, triangular outdoor swimming pool situated right on the seafront called the Jubilee Pool. It's the largest seawater lido in the UK, was built in 1935, is art deco in style and is a hugely popular local amenity throughout the summer months. I would have been interested in having a dip myself if it had been open and the temperature had been about twenty degrees warmer. In the current temperature, it was hard to imagine being able to swim without instantly dying of cold, but as we continued along the beach front we saw a middle-aged lady in a bikini emerge from the sea just like a much older, smaller, and saggier, version of Ursula Andress in *Dr. No*. We nearly bowed to her in admiration, but decided to pretend we hadn't noticed her. She was probably just an attention seeker. After all, what kind of person wears a bikini in Britain in April, let alone goes swimming in the sea in it? Huh!

We thought it would be a sensible idea to seek out some local knowledge about the best way to tackle Land's End, and the local office of the RNLI seemed like the obvious place to find it. We came across 'Patch', the coxswain, who put us on to a brilliant wind strength and sea state website called XC weather. The site has a map of Britain showing colour-coded arrows that indicate which direction the wind is blowing and what strength it is. For our purposes, blue and green equalled good, and pink and red equalled bad. If it was good enough for the RNLI, it was good enough for us.

In Newlyn, we were close to where the Penlee lifeboat disaster took place, which had happened as recently as 18th December 1981. We recalled hearing about it on the news. The lifeboat had been manned by eight volunteers from nearby Mousehole but, because of the dire conditions that day, only one volunteer from each family was allowed to go. The lifeboat was called out to go to the aid of a cargo ship called the *Union Star*, whose engines had failed just off the west Cornwall coast. The south-east winds were classified as Force 12, which is a terrifying hurricane level. The winds were gusting to 90 knots and the sea was reaching heights of sixty feet.

Initially, the RNLI crew had managed to save four people from the *Union Star* but, at some point later during the rescue, the swell tossed the lifeboat on to the deck of the cargo ship and all eight volunteer lifeboatmen and all the passengers and crew from the *Union Star* perished. Patch, the current coxswain, is the son of one of the volunteers who died that day in 1981.

When we heard the story we shuddered, knowing how scary even moderately choppy water can be at times. The courage of RNLI volunteers who risk their lives regularly in such unimaginable and terrible conditions is awesome.

What a fantastic service it is, and how reassuring it is to anyone who takes any kind of boat out on the sea that the RNLI are there to assist when things go wrong.

Newlyn to Milford Haven Across the Bristol Channel

We were so looking forward to welcoming the amiable Alex on board for extra company and to give us support during our next, quite daunting, passage. He also just happened to know everything there was to know about sailing, boats and engines. He finally arrived and we were able to discuss our passage plan in finer detail. We decided to grab the next weather window the following day before the inevitable arrival of the next bout of gales. Arriving in Newlyn was certainly the end of the beginning, and leaving Newlyn was the beginning of one of – if not the biggest – adventures of our lives. We'd been to the Isles of Scilly the previous year, but had never rounded Land's End before and never made a twenty-four-hour passage. It was going to make a big difference to our stress levels knowing that Alex was there to advise us if we needed it and also to give us some practical help.

Getting the timing right to go round Land's End is crucial. The tides can be very strong and, when heading in a northerly direction, it's important to catch the beginning of the north-going tide to get you safely round the headland and well away into the Bristol Channel before the tide turns against you. For a safer and more comfortable passage, the winds need to be moderate, especially if they are westerly; otherwise, there's a risk of being blown on to the very rocky lee shore. The coastline around Land's End is strewn with wrecks, but a huge number of them are from times when weather forecasts were made by assessing cloud formations, and aids to navigation like GPS and radar didn't exist.

Despite modern technology, shipping disasters still happen for a whole variety of reasons, like the engine failure of the *Union Star* in 1981. One of the most recent shipwrecks in the Land's End area was in March 2003. The RMS *Mulheim* was on passage from Cork in Ireland to Lubeck in Germany. The seas were moderate with occasional fog patches, so the weather wasn't a problem. The Chief Officer had got his trousers jammed in his chair and when he tried to stand up he managed to fall and knock himself unconscious. By the time he came round, it was too late to do anything to divert the boat from its fatal course. The Mulheim ended up hitting the rocks, but luckily all the crew were rescued. How would you ever be able to predict such an unfortunate incident? It just goes to show that anything can happen at sea, and it's not always down to the weather.

The trip to Milford Haven was going to take a minimum of twenty-four hours from ten o'clock on the Thursday morning to about ten o'clock on Friday morning if all went according to plan. We had previously decided not to try to break the journey anywhere, as the options were very limited. The north Cornish coast is fairly inhospitable to deep-keeled boats like ours, apart from Padstow, which you can still only enter at certain states of the tide and only a couple of hours either side of high water. Other than that, if we needed to take refuge anywhere, Lundy Island offered an anchorage, but only on the eastern side, which would be fine in order to avoid westerly winds, but not easterlies. The forecast was looking quite good, so, with added luck, we wouldn't need to run for cover. Newlyn to Milford Haven should be fairly straightforward.

We were excited, but more than a little anxious about crossing the Bristol Channel with its powerful tides and lack of refuge, and taking turns to be on watch overnight was going to be an entirely new experience for us. Sailing during the night hours was going to be the toughest part of the passage and Alex suggested that we worked out the rota to suit how each individual functioned best. I am known to be annoyingly chirpy very early in the morning just when Bob is at his worst, but Bob said he wasn't good late in the evening either and didn't seem convinced that he ever did have a 'best time'. We were secretly hoping that Alex was an all-night bird and might offer to do the whole night watch, so that we could sneak off to bed as normal and wake up in Milford Haven fresh as a daisy, just like you would on Stena Lines.

We cast off at ten o'clock the following morning in reasonable weather, wondering how it would feel and how we would cope. As we rounded the Runnel Stone, turned the engine off and hoisted the sails, we were accompanied by a group of dolphins. They were joyfully ducking and diving around the front of the boat as we carved our way northwards through gentle waves. It felt like a good omen. The weather was settled enough for us to sail through the narrow channel between the Longship's Lighthouse and Land's End itself. The fierce rocks either side would chew a boat up in no time in rougher conditions.

The rest of the day was a perfect day's sailing with the westerly wind resting constantly on our beam and our average speed being about 6 knots. We chatted and took turns to rest, had sandwiches for lunch and mentally prepared ourselves for the night sail as we forged on towards our destination.

It was all very satisfying until dinner. Unfortunately, back in Newlyn, I'd had the bright idea of going native by buying three extra large Cornish pasties for our evening meal. I thought pasties were the epitome of comfort food and would be the perfect thing to keep the stamina levels up during the night. Big mistake! Naturally, you'd expect a Cornish pasty made in Cornwall to be the finest quality, but these particular ones turned out to be greasy wedges of cheap gristle and a huge disappointment. I noticed that Alex ate his very slowly and probably didn't like to comment out of politeness, and I could only manage half of mine as the congealed pastry was become increasingly difficult to swallow. I never registered a verdict from Bob, spoken or implied, but the whole of the third pasty had disappeared, so I think he was so hungry that he'd have eaten a raw seagull if that's what was on offer.

After the pasty, I felt a bit sick for the next couple of hours, but luckily it coincided with me being off duty, so I wedged myself and my duvet under the cupboards next to my bunk and tried to exhale the yucky feeling away. By the time I was on duty, I was feeling back to normal and treated myself to a few stabilising digestive biscuits and a double Twix. When sailing at night, you do need to keep your spirits up at all times.

The night watch rota had been worked out so that one of us would be on deck for two hours while one slept within shouting distance, and the third one of us would be in their bunk and allowed to switch off totally. Then we'd swap round. The person within shouting distance is said to be on 'mother watch'; a state similar to lying half awake expecting to be disturbed by a screaming infant wanting a feed. Alex subsequently decided to make his bed in the saloon so, as far as I was concerned, he was always going to be within shouting distance. After the unfortunate pasty situation, though, I didn't want to risk waking him up by demanding regular feeds. I could easily pop down below quickly to get my own cheesy Wotsits.

My first solo night watch was between ten and midnight. I was alone on deck and secured in the cockpit by a harness, just in case. This was standard procedure on a night sail, and not a punishment for bad behaviour. We were still sailing on a beam reach with an average of 14 knots of wind, and it was an incredibly exciting feeling being propelled along purely by the wind yet not being able to see a thing. There was little to feel concerned about because there were only a couple of other ships visible on AIS and they were a long way off. I relished the adventurous feeling of being on deck alone in the dark and, while there were no panic situations, I felt completely in tune with the sounds of *Bella Rosa* swishing purposely through the water. It was a bit damp and chilly up in the cockpit on that April night, but the two hours went surprisingly quickly and then it was down below for a hot drink and a few hours' sleep.

My second shift was from four to six. I wanted to be the one that sailed from night-time into daytime, hoping that I may see a glorious sunrise, but, in the end, it turned out to be more of a series of progressively lightening shades of gloomy grey. It was good to see some colour contrast when I finally saw land, even though it was a dull shade of green. At 5.30 a.m., another school of dolphins appeared to keep me company and swam along with the boat for twenty minutes or so. It was a cheering sight on a cold and misty morning.

Despite the thick cloud cover, our night sail was straightforward, with consistent winds, very few gusts and no nasty surprises. The traffic in the Bristol Channel is always minimal, so, apart from a few fishing boats and the odd cargo ship in the distance, we had the place pretty much to ourselves. We arrived in Milford Haven almost exactly twenty-four hours after we had set off, having clocked up one hundred and forty-two nautical miles, pretty much all of it under sail. We were feeling a bit rough around the edges, but were infused with a great sense of achievement.

Milling About in Milford Haven

If you want a tattoo, Milford Haven is **the** place to get one. In the local newsagents, there was a section of shelf entirely devoted to publications such as *Tattoo World* and *What Tattoo?* magazine. There must be an awful lot to say about tattoos that the uninitiated can't even begin to imagine.

We left the marina on foot and walked along a fairly nondescript street looking for the town centre. We stopped a group of young people to ask for directions to it. "You're in it," they replied before convulsing with laughter. The marina was apparently the place to go for sophistication, if that's what we were after, so we vowed to look at it with new eyes on our return. On closer scrutiny, the marina amenities did offer levels of sophistication that were missing in the centre of Milford Haven. There was an Italian restaurant, a few souvenir shops selling objets d'art and endless things made from driftwood, and a café.

We were beginning to get into the swing of Milford Haven and went in search of some postcards. We'd planned to send one to my parents and our daughters from each port we visited and we were now at our sixth port of call. On our travels around the town centre, along with the tattoo parlours we came across a bowling alley and a Tesco, but it was impossible to find a shop that sold postcards of Milford Haven itself. There were postcards, but they were of everywhere else in the vicinity. Milford mustn't have fallen into the category of 'holiday destination', but, if you did happen to be there as a visitor – like we were – the postcard vendors thought it would look better to make out you were somewhere else by sending pictures of Broad Haven or the puffins on Skomer Island. Back at the marina, we managed to buy a postcard of the marina from a driftwood shop, and thought that would suffice, especially as the marina was where we ended up spending most of our time.

Initially, Alex was going to be sailing with us until we reached Dublin, but it looked like we were going to be stormbound in Milford Haven for several days at least. It would have been a complete waste of time for him to be hanging around with us in a tiny damp boat waiting for a chance to cross the Irish Sea. Bob and I now felt confident enough to tackle the crossing to Ireland on our own, so Alex headed back to his warm home and comfortable bed back in Hampshire, and left us to it.

By Day 2 we discovered that Milford Haven wasn't a cultural desert after all. We were going to be there for a few days, so needed some entertainment. We discovered a thriving theatre called the Torch Theatre and signed up for a pre theatre dinner of posh pie and chips in its modern restaurant, prior to watching *Who's Afraid of Rachel Roberts?* The play was of a very high standard, and we learned that the theatre had played host to many very well-known actors and actresses in the past. Discovering The Torch Theatre was the first of many heart-warming and life-affirming experiences around Britain of places that, on the surface, seemed unprepossessing but underneath had a rich seam of cultural, artistic and community enterprise. Don't judge a book by its cover, and don't listen when people tell you Britain is going to the dogs!

After the play, in order to continue mingling with the cream of Milford Haven society, we dropped into the Lord Nelson for a nightcap. We were met with suspicious looks, and thought it better to avoid eye contact. I was tempted to say loudly to the bartender, "My husband does have Welsh ancestry", as I think they must have understandably felt threatened by our sophisticated English demeanour. I accidentally smiled at someone on the way out, and was rewarded with a quick nod of the head. I think that if we ever wanted to live permanently in Milford Haven, with a little effort on our part they could eventually accept us.

Walking back to the boat in the dark along the cliff above the harbour, we could see the oil refineries along the estuary lit up like a Manhattan skyline. It looked almost magical at night, whereas, during the day, there was very little to see apart from a bleak, undulating landscape with a few industrial-looking constructions dotted around.

The weather continued to be diabolical. It was blowing a Force 10 out in the Irish Sea, and was raining cats and dogs where we were. To me, it was reminiscent of many childhood holidays in rented cottages, usually in wild and wet north Wales. If there had been a cinema in Milford, we would have gone to it and watched anything, just to get out, but Bob had managed to download an episode of *Mad Men* on the iPad, which we saved for the evening. He also managed to watch the Heineken Cup in full crackly colour. I played with my Brushes app and produced a still life entitled 'Bananas'. I was working towards doing an exotic summer scene from distant memory.

It hadn't been a difficult decision to stay put for the previous four days, as the weather down the whole length of the Irish Sea had been particularly unpleasant and crossing over it to Ireland was our next mission. We'd noticed that there were several other visitors in the Milford marina who had arrived at the same time as us, and none of them had left, which confirmed to us that we were right to stay. If we'd cottoned on to this fact earlier, we could have set up a small support group.

Ireland's large land mass protects the Irish Sea from

the big Atlantic swell but because it is relatively shallow and has strong tides the result is something known as the 'Irish Sea Chop'. Choppy sea is usually a short, steep sea, which can be uncomfortable and has the ability to leave you wallowing in the troughs and unable to gain momentum. (That is unless your boat is called *Bella Rosa*, the Wonder Boat). We didn't want to take any risks.

There was finally a glimmer of hope when the winds were forecast to die down long enough for us to cross with some peace of mind. We kept changing our minds about where we wanted to go first, but settled on Kilmore Quay on the south-west corner of southern Ireland because it was the shortest possible journey we could make, although it would still take us ten or eleven hours. That was long enough to feel exposed and vulnerable without any places of refuge. We phoned the harbour master at Kilmore Quay to check that there would be an available berth. He asked if we'd been there before and, when we said no, he said, "What took you so long?" The pilot book informed us that the Quarterdeck fish and chip shop was outstanding and the Silver Fox seafood restaurant was highly recommended. We loved the place before we'd even set foot in it.

In amongst all this passage planning, Bob had to resort to taking a course of antibiotics for an abscess on his gum. This was slightly disconcerting news for him because he would have to give up the booze for seven days just as we were about to sail to the land of Guinness and Jameson's. It would mean that his perspective on Ireland was going to be very different from the last time he went. This time, it would be in sharper definition and less blurred. I would have to hold the fort on that front and represent both of us.

As soon as the winds died down the following lunchtime, we left our marina and scuttled up to Dale, a sheltered, small bay at the mouth of Milford Haven. It felt oddly strange to leave because we now had a bit of a routine going and were beginning to feel like residents. In fact, on our last day in the marina, we met a lovely, retired gentleman, who was a genuine resident. He been living in the marina on his boat, *Laetitia*, for eighteen years, and was moored opposite *Bella Rosa*. Despite needing a walking stick on dry land, he still sailed his boat single-handedly from time to time. Respect!

Dale was a breath of fresh air with its spacious bay, a quaint waterside town and rolling countryside on one side and a few big cargo ships and oil refineries dotted about on the other. We didn't have time to leave the boat and go ashore but sat on deck to watch the sun go down. From Dale, we could slip off our mooring buoy at first light the following morning and head west with the wind behind us. The forecast was still promising.

Goodbye Wales, Hello Ireland!

Our passage to Kilmore Quay began at 5.50 a.m. We'd managed to pick up an Irish weather forecast, which seemed much lengthier than the average English ones. We were given the highs, the lows, the heights, the widths and much more minute detail about what was happening on the Irish side of the Irish Sea. They either weren't leaving anything to chance or Irish weather was genuinely more complex than English weather. The reader spoke rapidly and with such a strong Irish accent that it effectively scrambled half of what he was saying, and we started to lose concentration until being violently brought back to attention by the mention of fog banks. Fog banks had certainly not been mentioned during the previous night's forecast, but that forecast had been an English one.

Within an hour of setting off towards Ireland, visibility to the south of us was deteriorating rapidly and, within no time, we were consumed by dense fog. We could see that we were getting uncomfortably close to a cargo ship that showed up on the AIS as barely moving. We couldn't actually see the ship, as it was still a mile or so away, but, as we got closer to its apparent position on the AIS, it started to move very slowly towards us. Within seconds, the towering bow of the ship loomed up in the fog just ahead of us and caused our hearts to start pounding. It was a daunting sight. The ship's heading and speed meant that we were going to miss each other but, even so, we were dangerously close. They must have seen us on their radar and could have waited until we were safely past before setting off. The experience gave us quite a shock and was a reminder that it's best to give the big ships a very wide berth under all circumstances. With that in mind, our next escapade was to tackle the main shipping channel, knowing that it was foggy and there were five big cargo ships heading south towards us at 12 knots. It was becoming uncannily like something out of *Pirates of the Caribbean*.

We thought that we tackled the main shipping channel with aplomb by not getting crushed to a pulp by any of the five invisible oncoming ships. It was all thanks to being able to calculate their trajectories on our AIS, see how fast they were going and on what heading, factor in our own speed and heading, and then dodge behind them. At least this is what we assumed we were doing because, although we couldn't see a thing, we came out the other side completely unscathed. Result! Typically, the fog finally cleared only as we left the main shipping channel, but we were grateful for some respite and were able to have a well-earned perfect sail the rest of the way accompanied by more joyful, frolicking dolphins.

Kilmore Quay, Then Off to Arklow

Our stay in Kilmore Quay was to be brief because, by now, the weather had become more manageable and we were finally being offered a chance to make some significant headway. We were only going to stay in Kilmore Quay for one night and would head to Arklow up the east coast of Ireland the following day. Once we'd secured ourselves to our cosy pontoon, we still had plenty of time to have a look round the delightful small fishing town.

Ever conscious of our responsibility to the welfare of the wider world, our mission in Kilmore Quay was to help the Irish economy as much as possible. Eating out and shopping seemed to be the most practical way to go about it. We started the ball rolling by booking a table at the Silver Fox that evening to see if it lived up to its reputation, and I'm happy to report that it did. As we made our way round the town and got chatting to many of the locals, we realised that they all had genuinely serious concerns for their future as a community. Due to the dire economic situation in southern Ireland, tourist levels had dropped to a horrendously low level, and one of their two local pubs had been forced to close down. All the people we met were lovely, friendly and helpful, but there was an all-pervading sadness in the air. How would they keep going and what would the future hold?

We were spurred on even more to be as supportive as possible, so, although we didn't feel we could run to selling off *Bella Rosa* and donating the proceeds to the 'Help

Bail Ireland Out' fund, we did some more shopping. Bob bought himself some serious deck shoes and we bought an Irish courtesy flag for *Bella Rosa* as a present for staying so adorably the right way up. The local produce was not to be missed either, and we purchased several loaves of delicious Irish soda bread, a bag of industrial-sized scones and other delicious delicatessen goodies ready for the next day's passage to Arklow.

Before launching ourselves in the direction of Arklow and into the Irish Sea, we thought it would be wise to ferret out some local knowledge about the relevant tides and timings to ensure the safest possible passage round Carnsore Point, which is situated at the most south-easterly tip of Ireland. We popped into the local harbour master's office to ask for advice. He strongly recommended that we shouldn't leave before 13.00 the following day; otherwise, we'd be sitting between the two buoys flanking St Patrick's Bridge with the tide against us and going nowhere fast, or possibly even going backwards. St Patrick's Bridge was clearly visible from the harbour master's office window. We were grateful for the help, but wondered if they ever deliberately gave out wrong information in order to provide some light-hearted entertainment to brighten up a dull day.

St Patrick's Bridge is the name of the safe route through the extensive shallow sandbanks that frame the entrance to Kilmore Quay harbour. I wasn't sure what St Patrick had to do with a channel in the sea, but he did seem to have had a fair bit of influence in most places in Ireland, watery or otherwise. We'd only been in Ireland for one night and we'd already found ourselves following in the footsteps of a saint, even though it was by boat. I'd only ever heard of Jesus walking on water, but St Patrick must have had the gift as well.

We left Kilmore Quay at one o'clock after getting a

final update on the sea conditions and weather from the harbour master. All the forecasts had predicted a pleasant Force 3 to 4 – as did the harbour master – but they were all wrong and we ended up experiencing the Irish Sea Chop with winds gusting up to 25 knots for the following six and a half hours. The problems started as we were getting close to Carnsore Point and had to decide whether to take an inner passage between the shore and a long sandbank parallel to the shore or go outside the sandbank. It was a dilemma deciding what to do in an unknown territory. I was afraid of being trapped inside the sandbank and being battered by west-going breakers over the sandbank with no way to escape quickly, so we opted for the outside passage, which was at least at a safe distance from the lee shore. The sea outside the sandbanks was more exposed, so it could have been the case that we were experiencing a much more confused sea out there than we would have done if we'd taken the inner route. We would never know which route had been best. All we knew was that we eventually survived the Irish Sea Chop, and it was a force to be reckoned with. We also knew that the chop in even a slightly stronger wind with wind against tide would be highly unpleasant – if not dangerous – for a small boat like ours.

After we turned north towards Arklow, the wind was directly on the nose and, because we wanted to get there before dark, we ended up motor sailing all the way. Bob was heroically glued to the helm in order to work with the waves and help prevent us from slamming down into the frequent troughs. The 'chop' was relentless, and we felt like we were on one of those extreme experience simulators you find at public attractions; the difference being that they normally only last for about five minutes and not the best part of a day.

We arrived in Arklow cold, wet and exhausted to find that virtually all the potential moorings in the estuary had been taken by boats from the Welsh Motor Cruiser Association, who had arrived the previous day and were there for an upcoming rally. The marina had told us that they had space but, on investigation, there was only a tiny space available that was too narrow for *Bella Rosa*. We ended up poking the front half of the boat in and letting the back half of the boat stick out into the entrance channel. We tied her up as well as we could, and got stuck into a much-needed, pre-prepared shepherd's pie. Sometimes, it was easy to get beyond caring, especially when real fatigue set in.

The boat that later came in behind us was a solo sailor, who had had a very long and arduous passage and was so beyond caring that he just parked slap bang in the middle of the entrance channel. Luckily, no one else arrived that evening, and we were both leaving early the following morning so wouldn't be in each other's way.

It wasn't widely known among our friends that Bob was actually born with boats in his veins. Arklow is in fact the home of the renowned Tyrrell's boatyard, which is still owned and run by some of Bob's more distant relatives. The boatyard built *Gypsy Moth III* and another famous boat called *Asgard II*, which suffered the ignominious fate of sinking in the Bay of Biscay in 2007, but who's judging? We had planned on visiting the relatives, but our very late arrival and early departure the following morning put paid to that idea. We would have to save the visit for a future date. Next stop Dun Laoghaire.

No Time to Hang Around in Arklow, Dun Laoghaire was Beckoning

Getting up at five o'clock was tough after the previous day's escapades but we needed to leave Arklow by 6.00 a.m. to catch the north-going tide and would be in Dun Laoghaire before lunch. The winds were threatening to whip up again, and we didn't really fancy yet another day on the bouncy castle but desperately wanted to move on. We were keen to get there as soon as possible, have a shower, read our books and stretch our legs.

Forging our way up a grey and dismal Irish Sea, we found ourselves fairly short of entertainment and spent a good half an hour comparing how many layers of clothing we'd both been wearing during the last few days. That's how dull it was. Bob was currently wearing six layers and I was wearing five. As Bob normally wore shorts throughout the year – whatever the weather – the fact that he was wearing six layers of clothing plus trousers was evidence of how seriously cold it was. Who needs a barometer when you have a Bobometer? We were looking forward to a future time when we could wear less because it was quite hard to manoeuver around the boat dressed like stuffed marrows.

Arriving in Dublin Bay was an exciting experience. We were by now halfway up the coast of Ireland and knew we couldn't fail to enjoy being in the Dublin area. From previous visits, we knew Dublin was simultaneously both sophisticated and traditionally Irish. We were in the home of Irish culture, music, dancing, Jameson's and Guinness. Having spotted a virtual traffic control system on the chart, which incorporated a large, red and white striped buoy acting as a roundabout for big ships, we were cautious about entering the bay, but, although the ferries we saw were quite large, fast and frequent, we could easily avoid them if we sailed around the edge of the bay.

We could have travelled down the Liffey River and tied up in the centre of Dublin or gone slightly further north to Howth, but we'd chosen to stop in Dun Laoghaire, a well-to-do Georgian suburb of Dublin situated on the south side of the bay. Dublin life was only a short train ride away, but Dun Laoghaire had its own attractions by the bucketful and spread itself out along the rugged coastline that framed the bay. The marina itself was a joy to behold with its well-appointed location, sophisticated, biometric ID system and plush shower block. There was also the most luxurious and rare of marina facilities: a large and inviting bath.

After securing *Bella Rosa* to a generously long pontoon and allowing ourselves a short rest, we walked into Dun Laoghaire and dropped into a typical Irish bar to get stuck into the Guinness; the first and most obvious step needed when pursuing Irish culture. Bob had unilaterally decided that the odd drink wouldn't impact the effectiveness of his antibiotics. Wandering around the town afterwards, we came across our second Irish saint, this one going by the name of St Michael. There was something very familiar about the name, but we couldn't quite determine what it was. St Michael was an active entrepreneur as well as a saint, having set up a 'food hall', not unlike our very own Marks & Spencer. Ireland was truly turning out to be the land of the saints. Having had three consecutive days of sailing, we realised that we were very tired, so we bought a bag load of heavenly blessed food from St Michael's shop and headed back to *Bella Rosa* for a quiet evening of counting more clothing layers and an early night.

Doing Dublin

We discovered a convenient train service that ran from a station just across the road from the marina to the centre of Dublin. We had been to Dublin a few years previously prior to the credit crunch of 2008, and had found it to be a cool, trendy, vibrant and thriving place. We were concerned that the economic downturn would have destroyed some of Dublin's incredible Irish verve but, happily, it didn't seem to be affected at all and the city was still buzzing with life and optimism.

The Georgian period of the city was very much in evidence, although, apparently, a great deal of it had been destroyed during that architecturally barbaric period of the 1960s to make way for progress in the form of more modern blocks of housing and offices. Coming from the Georgian city of Bath, we felt very at home in Georgian Dublin, although it is a lot bigger and maybe a little bit sootier. We wanted to check out Number 29 Fitzwilliam Street, a typical Georgian house, which had been restored as a museum representing Dublin life between 1790 and 1820. One of the previous occupants of the house had been Mrs Olivia Beatty, who lived there with her seven children and her husband David, who was a wine merchant. They were just as paranoid about security as we are now, maybe even more so. The silver cutlery had to be counted after each meal and the doors needed to be firmly bolted to keep the riff-raff from raiding the place.

All in all, life in nineteenth-century Dublin didn't seem so different, apart from the fact that we all live longer now, can have burglar alarms installed and the staff aren't likely to steal the cutlery, as most of us don't have staff. As for riff-raff, you only need to go into the centre of Bath on a Saturday night to find that some things never change.

The sun was shining at last, but it was still very chilly. We walked for miles through the Georgian Quarter, Temple Bar, along the canal and back to the centre again to Grafton Street. I found myself continually inclined to pass people port to port and cross the road at right angles to the main traffic flow. That's the result of three weeks on a boat for you! In Grafton Street, we had a fabulously healthy lunch in the Avoca shop café. Avoca was my favourite shop in Dublin, with its beautiful, folky-style home wear, clothing and fabulous food department.

Dublin was currently playing host to a dance festival and a gay theatre festival. We didn't see much evidence of gay theatre apart from someone dressed as a tiger, prancing around to music in a very camp fashion. Bob reckoned that he could do a lot better, but I wasn't sure why he would want to because there was clearly no money in it. Purely by chance, we came across a free Irish dancing show being held in a small theatre in Temple Bar. It was all very 'Riverdance' and impressively agile. It was great to see such traditions being kept alive, especially by young people.

Wandering Along The Dalkey Wander

The Dalkey Wander is a circular walk of about seven kilometres along the coast to the east of Dun Laoghaire. Within minutes of embarking upon the walk, we stumbled across the perfect café for our morning coffee. It was aptly called the Promenade Café, because that is precisely where it was situated. When it comes to finding superior coffee shops, Bob is like a heat-seeking missile, especially around mid-morning. The cakes in the Promenade Café were so in the upper echelons of patisserie perfection that I felt compelled to put out an immediate severe cake warning to all my friends who shared my interest. In fact, I only tend to be friends with people who share my interest, so the broadcast went out to virtually everyone I knew who could be contacted. If we had been stormbound in Dun Laoghaire, it would have been no hardship because you could get a good lunch there as well.

The Dalkey Wander walk was a route full of interesting features. There was a forty-foot-deep swimming area hidden amidst the rugged, rock-strewn coast called the Forty Foot. (The Irish didn't mess around with fussy titles for things. They also have a coffee chain called Insomnia). People had been swimming in the Forty Foot all the year round for two hundred and fifty years, and Christmas Day was a particularly popular time to come. When we stopped to have a look, there was a small group of relatively elderly people either preparing to go in or just coming out. It was still only the beginning of May, and the water was freezing, and yet most of them were only wearing a swimsuit and a swimming hat. One lady in her eighties was wearing an additional pair of neoprene gloves, but you need a bit of extra comfort at that age. If we found ourselves still in Dun Laoghaire at the end of the week, we were thinking we might try to go in, but only wearing our industrial-strength wetsuits.

Dun Laoghaire To Ardglass

There's a large section of sea between just north of Dublin and south of Strangford Lough that barely has a tidal stream. The sea comes into the area from both sides of Ireland, and this is the area where the two tidal flows meet. The meeting of the tides is what neutralises the flow, although it still maintains quite a large tidal range. We were particularly looking forward to the passage to Ardglass because the weather forecast was looking very promising and the wind for once was predicted to be on the beam.

A few hours before we left, the forecast had begun to predict stronger and more northerly winds of Force 6 rising occasionally to a Force 7. If we stuck to our rule of 'never going out if a Force 7 was ever even mentioned briefly', we would have still been tied up in Portland marina. We wanted to make progress. We knew that, when considering all the variables, sometimes it can be perfectly manageable. In this case, although it was going to be a bit of a tiring ride, as it was to be a ten-hour trip, we had no tidal stream to contend with, and we knew that *Bella Rosa* was up to the challenge. The forecast was right about the wind strength, and it felt absolutely freezing, but the visibility was excellent, so we felt we'd made the right decision. Ardglass, our next stop, was in Northern Ireland.

For us, one of the best things about sailing was to be able to arrive somewhere by sea, just the two of us, and have everything we needed right there with us. We were frequently the only sailors out there on the ocean with only the occasional fishing boat or cargo ship to keep us company. Every day was a fresh experience, gave us a new purpose, and planning each new day was keeping us well occupied. Up to this point, we'd had some pretty difficult weather to deal with, but we'd already clocked up five hundred and sixty sea miles and were now in Northern Ireland in the middle of May. The sun was shining and Bob was having his morning cup of tea on deck. We were finally having a sense of how much better it was going to be when the weather did finally improve, which surely it would do in the near future. It had been really satisfying so far, but we still had so much to look forward to.

Ardglass To Bangor

Ardglass is a coastal village in County Down in Northern Ireland and a relatively important fishing harbour. The marina is small but well protected and safe, and open twenty-four hours a day despite the tricky little entrance and large tidal range. When the tide is out, the marina is surrounded by mud flats, and looks marooned apart from the narrow channel allowing access. The visibility was so good that we could see the faint outline of the Isle of Man in the distance. We went in search of a Guinness and then had dinner at the local golf club because none of the five local pubs served food. The golf club was very welcoming and the food was of a good standard. We had 'champ', which is a classic Irish dish of mashed potato and greens.

To our surprise, we found ourselves moored up on a pontoon next to another couple called Heather and Ed, who were also sailing round Britain. They'd travelled up from Swansea, and Ed was Welsh, so that was an immediate talking point for him and Bob, with Bob also having Welsh origins. They were sailing an aluminium-hulled yacht with a lifting keel called an Allures 44. The lifting keel would enable them to moor in drying harbours and sit on the mud when the tide went out. It would mean that they would have a more extensive choice of parking places than we did, but I preferred the idea that our keel was solidly attached to the rest of our boat, therefore having less to go wrong. They were the first 'normal' people we'd come across who were doing the same thing as us, and that was encouraging, as it was also their second time round. They'd obviously survived the first circumnavigation and had liked it so much that they were back for more.

We had our first lunch on deck in the marina in Ardglass under a clear blue sky in the warm sunshine. It had been hard to extract ourselves from the thermals, which by now were virtually fused to our skin, but we dug our shorts out and hoped that summer had finally arrived. The blast of sun and warmth was very short-lived. Three hours later, we were back in our thermals.

We were waiting to set off in the early afternoon to catch the north-going tide to take us up the coast and around the headland towards Belfast Lough and Bangor marina. When writing out a passage plan in the log book, it's customary to say you are heading *towards* a place rather than definitely going to a place. We were heading towards Belfast Lough, but if we didn't make it we'd never said we were actually going to Belfast Lough had we? So, neeeerrr. It's yet another nautical superstition about not tempting fate, and also not looking like a complete prat in the event of something unexpectedly going wrong or someone having done a substandard bit of navigation.

Our journey towards Belfast Lough was one of the most relaxing sails we'd had to date. The seas were calm, the winds gentle and there were terrific views of the verdant County Down coastline. It was so clear, that we could see the outline of the Mull of Kintyre in the distance.

The north-east corner of Ireland and the southern tip of the Mull of Kintyre are only approximately twenty-two miles apart, although, for us, safe haven to safe haven would be nearly double the distance. There was another bout of gales on the way, but we would be crossing the North Channel over to Scotland as soon as that had passed us by.

We sailed into Belfast Lough in the early evening and were stunned by the dramatic and moody scene that emerged before us. The huge, open expanse of water was peppered with reflections from the dazzling bursts of evening sunlight breaking through the great masses of cumulus clouds. The contrast of brooding, dark and shimmering light looked like something out of a Renaissance painting, and there we were, on our little boat, all on our own in the centre of it. It was spectacular.

Belfast Lough plays host to a continuous stream of commercial shipping as well as the occasional small fry like ourselves. There are several marinas dotted on either side of the lough, but we decided upon Bangor because there's a well-known, jolly folk song about it and the location sounded pretty. Bangor would also be a good jumping-off point for crossing the North Channel to Scotland, but Glenarm, a little further up the coast would be even better if the timing was right to go. It was all dependant on those two old favourites: the wind and the tide.

Bangor

In Bangor marina, Bob optimistically reached for his shorts again, and I got as far as opening my cupboard to check which T-shirts I'd brought with me in case there was another surprise attack of sunshine. When it did happen, it was often so fleeting that if we weren't ready and prepared we would miss the chance of doing that all-British thing of instantly stripping off virtually everything to bathe our lily-white skin in a few lukewarm rays, only to have to put everything back on again five minutes later. This was becoming a pattern. Once more, the thermals were reapplied and Bob reverted to his trousers and his five layers. Snow was forecast, but being so close to the wild, mountainous and remote shores of Scotland might have had something to do with it. It was lucky we'd brought along our thermally enhanced sailing kilts! We were certainly going to be needing them.

I found myself having a conversation with the fenders. I was a little concerned that the cold was beginning to leech into the deeper parts of my brain, but Fat Boy Fender and Fender Rosa reassured me that I was still perfectly sane, and I chose to believe them.

We went for a long walk along the National Trust coastline to a small place called Groomsport, where we came across an award-winning strudel café. It all sounded a bit Austrian to me but – what the hell –a cake is a cake, and the award-winning part needed investigating. Bob was struck by the fact that the café even had a mission statement, which was the first time he'd ever come across that in a mere café. The mission statement must have worked for them because they won the County Down Casual Eating Award and were about to go to Dublin to compete in the all-Ireland finals. For Bob, this reference to the corporate world got him thinking about how it could learn something from the sailing world. The marinas we'd visited so far had provided us with a fantastic level of customer service, and the man in the Bangor marina office was at the top of our list of helpful people. Nothing was too much trouble for him from recommending restaurants to finding Bob a local dentist.

Our trip hadn't begun as a prolonged cake fest round Britain but was turning into one. We could only blame the weather and the need for regular calorific comfort. We also decided to blame the Irish, who produce some of the best bakery to be found anywhere. If we spent much longer in Ireland, we'd be having to get our companionway opening enlarged or be in danger of spending the rest of the journey blobbing out on deck. The strudel was delicious, and so was the rhubarb scone, and, Bob, being a regular gannet, ate most of both. He was always able to eat for two and get away with it. Life can be so unfair.

Having exhausted ourselves eating, we headed back to the boat via Bangor town centre, but most of the shops were closed and heavily shuttered. The police station was surrounded by ten-foot-high grills and barbed wire. It was all clearly a throwback to the Troubles. We were told that Bangor had escaped much of the sectarian violence during the Troubles, but there were still multiple killings, car bombs, incendiary devices and extensive damage done to many of the shops and a few of the local churches. It was hard to imagine such violence occurring in a place that had such a similar identity to home, and hard to imagine the feeling of being physically at risk on a daily basis.

Despite the threatening atmosphere created by

everything being shuttered up, Bangor turned out to be an otherwise attractive town and still retains a Victorian seaside feel to it. During the working week, when the shops were open and active, the atmosphere changed dramatically to that of a perfectly normal British town. Tourism was being heavily promoted and we thought it should do very well because Bangor and its environs had much to offer. If only the weather could be more predictable!

Bangor To Glenarm

We didn't want to miss the opportunity to cross from the north-eastern corner of Ireland to the south end of the Mull of Kintyre in Scotland to be in Tarbert in time to meet up with our friends, Louise and Peter. They were on a birdwatching holiday in the area and would be leaving soon. There were more gales predicted, so we gave the *Titanic* exhibition in Belfast a miss and carried on up towards Glenarm in order to be ready to cross the North Channel when the weather was milder with a westerly wind.

The journey to Glenarm was only four and a half hours, which by our standards was a quick hop up the coast. Despite being a shortish journey, it was a tedious one. We were blighted by a succession of squally showers with intermittent gusts of over 30 knots and winds that suddenly dropped right down to 12 knots at other times. We were constantly having to adjust the sails to accommodate the fluctuating wind, and our heads were throbbing with all the concentration that was needed.

I took my hat off for a bit to stop my brain from overheating. When not wearing a hat – which didn't happen often – my hair usually blew in the same direction as the prevailing wind and stayed there long after the wind had died down. It was normal for me to have an asymmetric hairdo but by the time we reached Glenarm the confused winds had given me a huge, Dallas-style bouffant, enough to make even Joan Collins envious. I quite liked my wild, sailing woman persona and, in any case, we were intrepid travellers shortly to set sail for Scotland, the land of wild hairdos, whisky and William Wallace. I felt sure we would be welcomed as kindred spirits.

We were very relieved to arrive in Glenarm intact, and were greeted by a very waggy spaniel and his lovely, helpful (harbour) master, who gave us a full brochure's worth of information about his tiny town. There was a shop and two pubs, but neither of them served food, so it was to be Remoska time again that evening. We'd planned to have a full day off the next day and immerse ourselves in the luscious Irish countryside for one last time. Just for a change, we would be on the lookout for a chance to indulge in one last Irish cake before moving on to Scottish cakes, or did I mean Scotland?

We could see the outline of the Mull of Kintyre from the Glenarm marina, and were thrilled to think that we'd come this far in only four weeks. We had high expectations that the Western Isles of Scotland would be a brilliant cruising ground. The scenery was renowned to be stunning, and the vast number of island communities meant that we would be able to anchor among them in secluded little bays and coves. That was what sailing was all about.

The Giant's Causeway and Bushmills

The Irish Sea Chop was putting on another grand performance outside Glenarm marina. I doubt we would have been able to leave the harbour safely even if we had wanted to. The north-east wind was blowing straight into the entrance and causing plenty of that coastal turmoil that I'd been reading about. It was just as well that we'd decided to have a whole day off.

The strong winds didn't put us off taking a bus ride along one of the most dramatic coastlines we'd ever seen. The coastal road rose up to hundreds of feet above sea level, and there were views for miles through the glens of County Antrim, along the rocky, undulating coastline and over to the Mull of Kintyre. The bus journey took an hour and forty-five minutes, which is a long time to be on an ordinary bus, but we were on no ordinary bus route. It was one long, continuous feast for the eyes, and we spent the whole time staring out of the window, not wanting to miss a square foot of the luscious scenery. We were on our way to see the famous Giant's Causeway, which was situated near the north-east corner of the mainland.

The Giant's Causeway is the most popular tourist attraction in Ireland and was designated a World Heritage site in 1986. It's an area of 40,000 interlocking basalt columns, which – local legend tells – were a result of a volcanic eruption. Of course, the truth is that the columns are the remains of a causeway built by an Irish giant endearingly named Finn MacCool. Finn MacCool was challenged to a fight by a Scottish giant more boringly called Benandonner. Finn MacCool built the causeway across the North Channel so that they could meet in the middle, which was very accommodating and community spirited of him. The finer detail and the outcome of the battle is a bit of a grey area and there are, of course, several versions, but one version is that Benandonner didn't do too well in the ensuing battle and fled back home, destroying the causeway behind him. To back this theory up, there are identical basalt columns at Fingal's Cave on the Scottish Isle of Staffa. What more proof do we need?

We walked down the designated path among hordes of foreign tourists, and eventually reached the sea edge. Assuming this was the Causeway, my initial reaction was of deep disappointment, until we realised that we were looking in completely the wrong direction. This was all due to being wrongly influenced by a cluster of Japanese tourists, who were manically taking pictures of a very ordinary pile of rocks. When we twigged we'd made a mistake, we left the enthusiastic Japanese to it, and carried on for another quarter of a mile before reaching the real thing.

The proper Giant's Causeway genuinely lived up to expectations. It looked like someone had taken an ordinary rocky coastline photograph and transformed it with the pixelating function on Photoshop. Maybe that's where the idea of pixelating first came from? What better evidence that all the best creative ideas originate in nature?

Having absorbed enough geological phenomena, and several scones at the National Trust café, our next port of call was the Bushmills distillery. The distillery was situated just down the road from the Giant's Causeway, so perfectly close by for the pressed-for-time tourist. Bob – being a whisky connoisseur – was very excited, as the distillery visit was the main reason he'd signed up for this trip. The tour only took forty minutes, which meant that we could get to taste the stuff within a reasonable time of arriving. I don't particularly like whisky, so I chose the hot toddy option, which had cinnamon and sugar in it, and Bob went for the twelve-year-old malt. Bob's view was that I was a complete Philistine, and he went to sit at a separate table to avoid contamination by hot toddy and having to mix with plebs like me. A large bottle of the twelve-year-old malt joined us for the bus ride back to Glenarm and ended up with all the other bottles in the secret drinks cabinet on the boat.

Navigating the North Channel

Once off the bus in Glenarm, we decided that we should visit one last Irish pub before leaving the next day for Scotland. On our return from the pub, a fellow sailor called George from a nearby boat called the *Cuan Fisher* came over to tell us that our topping lift halyard had come unattached earlier that day and was flying about, threatening to whack some unsuspecting person on the head. He'd secured it for us and told us how to avoid it coming off again. That's the kind of camaraderie you get among the sailing community, and, once an acquaintance has been established, it's often not long before a prolonged chat ensues or an invitation is issued. That's exactly what happened with George.

Later that evening after our dinner, we strolled down the pontoon and hailed George. It turned out that George was sailing with his first mate, John, a deep sea fisherman turned second-hand car salesman and linked or related to George through the latter's daughter. George and John were both up from Bangor, knew the area inside out and were about to head towards Skye and beyond.

The evening was a delight, drinking red wine and whisky with the heating on full blast in George's lovely, cosy, teak-lined saloon. It was also invaluable to get the endless tips about where to go and what to see in the Western Isles of Scotland. They not only had bags of sailing experience between them but were full of great seafaring tales that they'd collected over many years. George was in his seventies and said that he was feeling a bit too old and decrepit to sail single-handedly anymore. These days, he took John or another younger friend with him on his expeditions to do all the harder deck work, and usually motor sailed just with the mainsail up to minimise the hard work. His boat also had an enclosed wheelhouse, immune to the elements. We didn't realise boats like that existed and were momentarily a bit envious before feeling a bit disloyal to *Bella Rosa*. We stayed late, relishing the company and the craic, and were sorry to leave, but they were off quite early the following morning and George needed his sleep.

I popped my head up early the following morning when I heard the rumble of a boat engine and saw George ensconced in his wheelhouse and John on deck in what looked like Arctic clothing, tidying up the fenders and warps. They were too engrossed in the process of leaving to notice me, so I wasn't able to wave, but I felt fondly towards our new friends as I watched the *Cuan Fisher* head out into the vast open space of the Irish Sea.

We set off a little later and had intended to go to Campbeltown, which was the nearest Scottish port from Glenarm, but on the way we decided to go a bit further to Lamlash Bay on the Isle of Arran to get a few more sea miles under our belts. The sea was flat calm and the air was still but the sky was heavy with dull, grey clouds and the visibility was very poor. It was still by far the easiest passage we'd had since starting the trip, but we couldn't see much of Scotland until we were within a few miles of it. It was still freezing cold, and the scenery continued to be the whole spectrum of shades of grey, which made it hard to take a good photo. We located Arran, found ourselves a convenient mooring buoy in the bay and felt elated to have arrived in bonny Scotland, even if we had yet to set foot in it!

Our arrival in Lamlash Bay coincided with dinner time. Fortunately, Bob had planned well ahead and had made en route a delicious and comforting oven-baked fish dish, which included posh baked beans. We accompanied it with an equally comforting bottle of wine to assist with the thawing-out process. When you wake up every day to weather that should only belong in February in the Arctic tundra, and your breath appears as plumes of white vapour even when you're still in bed, what keeps you going is good, hot, simple food. Bob's new self-appointed role in life was to ensure that we were well fed at all times, and in Lamlash Bay he came up trumps yet again!

Arran to Tarbert

The journey from Arran to Tarbert was all Scotch mist and motoring. We couldn't see much and, as there was no wind, we couldn't sail either. Despite the general gloom, when Tarbert finally appeared it looked very pretty and inviting. We planned on treating ourselves to two nights in a hotel or bed and breakfast to thaw out properly, and looked forward to a proper bed and a luxurious hot bubble bath.

We checked out the Anchor Hotel, who offered us the only room they had left, which, we were told, had a sea view. We trudged up five flights of stairs to have a look. We weren't that bothered about the sea view – given that we'd had a continuous one on the boat – but there was no view at all unless you stood on a chair to look through a very high window across a flat roof covered in seagull mess. More importantly, it only had a shower. The man on reception was very lucky we were polite to him when we returned his key. He nearly ended up being pinned to his own noticeboard, given the disappointment we felt.

The desperate craving for a bath passed, because it had to, and we were forced to take the marina shower option instead. The shower option was an initial ten minutes of a scalding hot dribble of water down a cold, tiled wall, in a room resembling a public convenience with some of the chill taken off. After ten minutes, it did work properly, but I didn't dare risk trying to wash my hair in case it reverted back to a boiling dribble. I booked into a local hairdresser for a wash and blow-dry at less than half the price of the same thing at home. It may get colder the further north you get, but some things also get cheaper, and that includes hairdressers and marina fees. In John O'Groats, they probably pay people to have their hair blow-dried.

Tarbert is a charming little harbour tucked into the hillside of the Mull of Kintyre. It's one of the most sheltered harbours in the lower Western Isles and is accessible to sailing boats at any time. We were beginning to see more yachts out and about in the firths, which was a welcome change from being virtually alone. On our first night in Tarbert, we had a yacht's worth of male Liverpudlians as neighbours, and a small boat load of students from the University of Strathclyde. The range of types of people who sail is wide and constantly surprising. Perhaps an adventurous spirit, a touch of madness and the joy of being able to escape the crowds out on the ocean are some of the common denominators. However did the world of sailing pass me by when I was younger?

The highlight of our week was meeting up with our friends, Louise and Peter Virley, from Bath. They were up in the area on holiday and just happened to be passing through Tarbert at the time we were there. They were on their way to the Trossachs after having spent a few days on the Isle of Islay, birdwatching and breathing fresh, Scottish air. We had a memorable seafood lunch at the Starfish Restaurant in Tarbert and caught up on all the news from home. They had been suffering the same cold weather as we had but were staying in a hotel with a bath. Bob and I just about managed to keep smiling as we battled with extreme bath envy. They seemed impressed by the fact that we still appeared to be relatively sane after a tough month at sea. Appearances can be deceptive. It was good to see old friends and we felt rather sad when they left.

The Beautiful Kyles of Bute

We'd been bracing ourselves for a further seven weeks of interminable cold weather, and were on the verge of parcelling up all our summer clothes and sending them home, when, hallelujah!, the sort of day we'd been hoping for finally arrived. We'd waited five whole weeks for the pleasure of waking up to clear blue skies and to experience the joy of sailing peacefully through gently rippling waters with the warm sun on our backs. What a difference a day makes. This was Scotland at its best.

Tarbert is just a short hop away from the Kyles of Bute, which were on our list of desirable destinations. The Kyles of Bute are not a chavilly named Scottish boy band but are in fact two natural waterways that join at the top end to form a V shape. Our life at sea meant that we had oodles of available time to investigate the minutiae of everyday life, so we Googled the meaning of Kyle and discovered that in Scotland it means a strait or a channel. The name 'Kyle' (singular) apparently exists in other places in Scotland, as in the Kyle of Lochalsh, and it can be also found in America, as, for instance, Clint Eastwood's jazz-playing son, Kyle Eastwood. I may be wrong, but it seems that we were sailing round the only Kyles (plural) in the whole world! You can't get much more adventurous than that. To all of the younger generation of travellers, stick that in your gap year and smoke it!

We tootled (for we were in a frivolous and jocular mood, which allowed for tootling) up the western leg of the Kyles, to find one of the numerous visitor buoys dotted along the route, where we were going to stop for the night. The improved weather conditions must have inspired other yacht owners to venture out because the Kyles could almost be described as being 'busy'. The scenery was stunningly beautiful and we were so glad we didn't miss out on seeing this area properly.

We moored on a buoy owned by the Kames Hotel near the apex of the West and East Kyles, and rowed ashore for a walk and a beer at the hotel. The mooring buoys were free to customers using the hotel bar, which seemed like a fair deal to us, particularly as we would have ended up there anyway. The hotel bar was geared up for a fiftieth birthday party that evening and, for some unknown reason, was dressed out like a Las Vegas wedding parlour. We assumed it was meant to be ironic. It wasn't closed to the public until later on that evening, so we took our drinks to an available cosy corner and watched the Heineken rugby cup final on their huge TV. Bob was deliriously happy.

Otter Ferry and Loch Fyne

It turned out that Loch Fyne isn't just a well known chain of fish restaurants. We spent the whole day sailing all around it and ended up in a tiny place called Otter Ferry, where there is a pub called the Oyster Catcher and more free mooring buoys. The water was as flat as a pancake, so we decided against going to all the trouble of attaching the outboard motor to the dinghy, and rowed in to shore instead. At the pub, they were holding a small classic car and motorcycle convention, and Bob got into a long discussion about a 1914 James motorbike, which the owner still used to travel to and from work. I didn't realise Bob was that interested in motorbikes but I think after spending five weeks with mainly me he just wanted an independent, manly conversation of his own. So as not to be entirely left out, I threw in the comment "Nice bike" at one point, only to have four pairs of male eyes swivel briefly in my direction before resuming what sounded to me like a lot of grunting between words like 'sump' and 'clutch'. After tearing Bob away from his new bosom buddies, we had a respectable fish and chip dinner in the pub before rowing back to the boat just as the sun was beginning to set.

The late evening was still very warm and couldn't have been more tranquil. If we could only have chosen to have good weather in one place, this was where we would have wanted it. It was almost impossible to describe the ethereal beauty of Otter Ferry, perched at the entrance to Loch Fyne and suspended there in a magical and meditative stillness.

We were so grateful to have a break from the cold

and often difficult conditions we'd experienced up to this point. Having heard that midges are a common pest in Scotland in the summer, we assumed that the sudden good weather had taken them by surprise, and that's why they hadn't made an appearance yet. We were moored at the edge of a huge, beautiful loch, watching a deep pink sunset, accompanied by only one other yacht in a sunny, warm, midge-free Scotland. How lucky can you get?

A Visit to Inverary

It was another glorious day in Loch Fyne. We motored in an easterly direction along the length of the loch to a well-known tourist destination called Inverary. We anchored offshore and rowed in to mingle with the proletariat and to see the castle. It's no wonder that Inverary attracts visitors from all over the world because it has everything you'd expect to see in a small, Scottish rural town. There is a sense of real history there with its old wonky buildings, the lochside location and the imposing castle at the centre of things.

Inverary Castle is a compact, square-shaped, olive green building with four corner turrets. Apart from the room with the vast collection of evil-looking weaponry, it was surprisingly homely and still frequently lived in by the family. The thirteenth Duke and Duchess of Argyll were in residence and we saw them both from a distance. They looked decidedly ordinary apart from the fact that the Duchess was wearing very sturdy brogues, thick, woolly tights and was swathed in Campbell tartan. It was the distinctive tartan that gave the game away as we watched her walking round, checking on the running of the shop and café. We spotted the Duke going through a private set of doors at the back of the castle. He was completely tartan free in a polo shirt and chinos, but we knew it was him because we'd seen a large collection of family photographs in the drawing room.

I was surprised and a little disappointed to see from the photos that the Duke and Duchess had allowed *Hello!*

magazine to cover their wedding. It's clearly not just the preserve of attention-seeking celebrities. These days, it seems that your average aristocrat can be just as strapped for cash as everyone else and have much bigger maintenance bills. At least they hadn't opened a safari park on site. We bought some sandwiches for lunch in the town and also bought a few bags of Scottish-made soaps and lotions to give to people as presents when we got home.

At the end of the day, we returned to Otter Ferry to moor overnight ready for an early start the following morning to negotiate the Crinan Canal.

Otter Ferry to Ardfern Via the Crinan Canal

Having managed successfully to negotiate a few large canals in Holland when we first brought *Bella Rosa* home, we were fairly upbeat about tackling the Crinan. The Crinan Canal was completed in 1801 and is a nine-mile-long navigable channel between the Clyde and the Inner Hebrides. It was built to provide a safe route and access to the Western Isles and was used extensively by Clyde Puffa cargo vessels, which were designed specifically to fit the narrow Forth and Clyde, and Crinan canals. Coal and general supplies were shipped northwards and they returned with whisky and other produce.

The Crinan Canal was a lifeline in those days but now is mainly used by many leisure vessels such as ourselves. It connects Ardrishaig with the small town of Crinan and would enable us to avoid going right the way round the exposed Kintyre Peninsula to get to the more northerly parts of Scotland. We'd heard that the Crinan Canal is dubbed 'the world's most beautiful short cut', and that it was quite special. We were so looking forward to sailing along an inland waterway for a change without having to worry about tides and swell. We left Otter Ferry in high spirits.

There are sixteen locks along the Crinan and it's possible to book an assisted passage, which we did. We thought that our paid-for assistant was the physically enthusiastic chap in a tatty bush hat, who was with us from the start, and went out of his way to help us by taking our lines and moving every single lock gate for us. The locks in the Crinan were all manually operated, and a lot of strength was needed to move the huge, heavy lock gates. It was hard labour and we didn't know how we could have possibly managed on our own.

Along the whole route, we were accompanied by one other yachtload of men, who had just recently participated in the Three Peaks Yacht race. The race involves sailing (motoring isn't allowed) from Barmouth to Fort William and stopping at convenient points to enable two of the crew members to run up each of the highest peaks in England, Wales and Scotland over three to four days. Cycling comes into it somewhere as well, which makes it one of the oldest extreme multi-sport races in the world. Apparently, it's the equivalent of running three marathons.

We didn't realise until we arrived in Crinan that our abnormally agile, bush-hatted assistant was actually a crew member from the other yacht. He had in fact been an active participant in the Three Peaks race, and was therefore not a normal human being at all but a bionic superhero. What luck that our official assistant hadn't shown up. Even with all the help from the bionic man, it was still very hard work tying up and untying the warps and trying not to bash into the rough walls of the locks or the other yachts.

We'd had high hopes of the Crinan but our appreciation of the surrounding area was probably coloured by the trauma of the exhausting slog through the sixteen locks. We were unimpressed. The scenery – when we had time to look at it – didn't seem particularly striking or exceptional in any way, although it was certainly quite pretty. The vistas did seem to improve as we approached the Crinan end of the canal but it could have been more the sense of relief at having nearly finished than the nature of the countryside. The landscape towards Crinan opened up into what looked remarkably like the flat open plains of Africa, but without the wildebeest. Our verdict was that the best way to see the Crinan Canal is on foot or by bike.

Our journey through the Crinan had taken seven and a half hours, with little time to relax and eat or drink properly. We were mighty glad it was all over. When we finally left the last of the sixteen locks to rejoin the open sea, the tide was with us, which had been part of the plan. Wrung out with exhaustion, we speedily headed on up Loch Craignish to take refuge in the very civilised Ardfern marina.

On our arrival at Ardfern marina, a helpful man appeared from a very impressive nearby motorboat, offering to take our lines, which was just as well, given the mess we were making of the parking. Having got no energy left for cooking anything which would have involved too much effort at that stage, we ate a couple of emergency cans of Marks & Spencer's curry for dinner, and just sat in a peaceful stupor. We had fleeting thoughts about what the Caledonian Canal would be like, but we didn't like to think too far ahead. Little did we know then that our experience in the Crinan Canal was to play a large part in our eventual decision to make quite dramatic changes to our route plans.

Arfern to Oban

The next part of our trip was turning into an entirely different experience. The weather had transformed the landscape and the sea into a Mediterranean idyll, but with all the extra character that Britain offers and without the dodgy tavernas. The beauty of the tranquil Western Isles was dreamlike and surreal, and at times rendered us quite speechless. We found ourselves saying "Just amazing!" and shaking our heads a lot!

The added dimension for us was being able to appreciate the isles from the sea. We travelled among them freely and independently, and were able to admire their qualities from many angles. We came across tiny sheltered anchorages, solitary dwellings that appeared out of nowhere, an occasional castle or a grand Scottish manse perched on a headland, and sometimes a pretty little town with a harbour. Nothing that we'd ever done before even came close to what we were experiencing during these days.

The route from Arfern to Oban passes through an area renowned as a tidal nightmare. The area incorporates the notorious Gulf of Corryvreckan. The gulf is an area of sea between two islands, which sometimes throws up a large whirlpool of water that can suck you down into the depths of the ocean without a trace, Yikes! At times, there can be 8 knots of tide running through the gulf, usually in the opposite direction of where you want to go. At springs and certain states of the tide, the whole area can be highly dangerous for a small yacht. We didn't need to pass through the actual gulf, only pass along one side of it, but the tides surrounding it can also run at angles to each other and they create many areas of tricky overfalls and eddies. It's a minefield.

On the day we wanted to pass through the area, the weather conditions were good. It was spot on springs though, which meant that tidal streams were running at their strongest. The previous evening, I'd spent about two hours scrutinising all the relevant pilot books and charts, and felt confident that with a well-worked-out passage plan there would be little risk. I plotted about twelve closely-spaced waypoints on the chart to see us safely through the tide rips and rocks all the way to Oban.

Despite being armed with the best possible passage plan, we were still apprehensive about having to pass so near to the Gulf of Corryvreckan. However much checking and double checking you do, there can always be unexpected things that take you by surprise, especially when cruising in unfamiliar waters. Even though the weather was calm and clear, we could see many areas of turbulence in the water, although the gulf itself looked positively innocent. With all being seemingly under control, I went down below to prepare some sandwiches for lunch, and left Bob in charge.

When I came back on deck, it was clear that we were being slowly sucked off course towards the gulf and Bob hadn't noticed – he'd been reading the paper on his iPad. Luckily, we hadn't drifted too far and were able to accelerate hard and get back on track. It was probably a good job that I'd surfaced when I did; otherwise, who knows where we could have ended up. Possibly in the lost city of Atlantis! You can't mess with a determined tide!

As we approached Fladda at the northern end of the Sound of Luing, we were surrounded by a whole series of small, unavoidable whirlpools. Whirlpools often occur when a strong main tidal flow borders an eddy heading in the opposite direction. This is a very common occurrence at springs. We sailed on through them and hoped for the best, and, while the steering felt odd with all the turbulence passing under the hull, we didn't feel ourselves to be in any serious danger. We could only imagine what it would be like to try to sail through that region in anything other than calm weather. It was something to be avoided, we thought, and felt relieved that we'd had the good fortune to be able to pass through in clement conditions.

At the far end of the well-protected Sound of Kerrera, we beheld a wondrous vision in the form of the well-known Scottish resort town of Oban. Here, we would find a much desired refuge from whirlpools and the like and possibly a WHSmith's. What a heart-warming thought that was.

Oban is informally known as the 'gateway to the isles' and also 'the seafood capital of Scotland'. We couldn't wait to check out the gateway and – more importantly – the seafood. There is a very prominent building called Macaig's tower overlooking the town. It was built in the late 1800s by a wealthy philanthropic banker called John Stuart Macaig to provide a lasting monument to his family and to create work for the local stonemasons. He got the idea for the design from the Colosseum in Rome, which just happens to be the largest amphitheatre in the world and was built by an emperor in AD 70. Macaig clearly had big ideas about his status in Oban as he'd also planned to incorporate a museum, an art gallery and lots of stone statues of himself and his family. He unfortunately died without finishing his project, and only the outer walls of the structure were completed. Nowadays, there is a public garden up there and the views are stunning.

There were some big Caledonian MacBrayne ferries moored on the town quay, a galleon, a large yacht belonging to the Ocean Youth Trust of Scotland and lots of other smaller commercial boats dotted about. We chugged around the main harbour but there were no obvious mooring spots for visiting yachts. From the charts, we could see that Ardantrive Bay, just off the island of Kerrera, opposite Oban, is home to a small marina. This seemed like the right place to go. There were a few vacant visitor buoys in the bay next to the marina, so we picked one up for the night rather than tackle a pontoon. Once on the buoy, we realised that we'd actually arrived at one of the marinas where we'd arranged to have our mail sent on. How exciting the prospect of collecting over a month's worth of mail the following morning, even if a lot of it turned out to be junk or bills we'd forgotten to put on direct debit.

Tobermory

To get from Kerrera to Oban, you have to catch a cute little ferry. We were only spending one morning in Oban before setting off to the picturesque and colourful town of Tobermory on the Isle of Skye. Most of our time was spent stocking up with provisions but a refreshing stroll round Waterstones and Boots was high on the agenda. Having a prolonged break from the regular fixtures of our normal daily life had been quite liberating for a while, but we were now beginning to crave the comfort of our familiar haunts. After a satisfying session in the aforementioned shops, we scoured the 'seafood capital' for a good fishmonger to buy some locally caught fish. We bought bulk salmon, mackerel and haddock before remembering that our fridge was the size of a biscuit tin. Eventually, Bob did manage to squeeze it all in after a major reshuffle, but we would have to eat on board for the next three nights at least before it all started to rot.

Tobermory was always going to be one of our most significant destinations, not least because it was while reading Libby Purves' description of it in *A Summer's Grace* that I was seduced by the idea that I also wanted to sail round Britain. Tobermory, in our original plan, was also going to be the furthest point north for us before we turned south again to Fort William to forge the Caledonian Canal. It was while we were wandering around Oban that we began to consider the possibility of going beyond Tobermory and ultimately sailing right round the top of mainland Britain. The idea of sailing right round the top hadn't, up to this point, been on our agenda at all, as we deemed it way beyond our capabilities and far too scary. Would our accumulated experience to date be enough to see us through? Would we taking too big a risk?

Having drastically been put off canals after our Crinan experience, and having begun to think we might seriously regret it if we missed the chance of going round the top, we began to investigate what it would involve. If we managed to pull it off successfully, it would be an enormous achievement for us relatively novice sailors, and an opportunity that would be unlikely to materialise ever again. We knew that the route around Cape Wrath is very exposed to the elements, and we'd read that huge seas can build up very quickly. There was always going to be an element of risk and anxiety, especially for first timers like ourselves, but we decided that we could slowly edge our way north beyond Tobermory to test our feelings, and we didn't need to fully commit until we were at the last safe harbour just south of Cape Wrath. We were in the fortunate position of knowing that we would be able to turn back at any time but had a sneaking suspicion that we wouldn't. It was by now becoming too enticing a proposition to quit.

The whole venture seemed like a wonderful idea until I read a section in *Reeds Almanac* about the Pentland Firth, which is the six-and-a-half-mile-wide stretch of water between the Orkneys and mainland Scotland. The Pentland Firth is the equivalent of Cape Wrath at the eastern side of the northern coast of mainland Scotland, and its existence hadn't even entered my consciousness until this point due to being completely irrelevant to our venture. If we were to round the Wrath, it would unfortunately become highly relevant. The quote from *Reeds Almanac* made sailing through the Firth sound like an impossible feat. It stated that "the Pentland Firth is a dangerous area for all craft... tidal streams reach 9 to 12 knots between Pentland Skerries and Duncansby Head. The resultant dangerous seas, very strong eddies and violent races should be avoided by yachts at all costs". After reading that, the decide-o-meter not surprisingly swung dramatically in the direction of reverting back to Plan A, which was to chop off the whole top of Scotland by travelling via the Caledonian Canal.

However much we tried to convince ourselves otherwise, we could not let the full circumnavigation idea go, but remembered that we still didn't have to commit until much later. I had a quick look at the Marine Traffic website, which has little symbols that show the position of all registered boats in current transit. There were very few registered boats passing through the Pentland Firth except a few cargo ships and a fifty-three-metre galleon, and they were all of Swedish extraction anyway, which frankly didn't represent normality. There were no small yachts to be seen at the time I looked but we'd heard that many normal people sail round perfectly safely – and survive intact – and Libby Purves was one of them. Maybe the secret was to go via the Orkneys?

After another look at the charts, taking the route via the Orkneys seemed like the only viable option for us. It looked like it was possible to sail through the Scapa Flow in the centre of the Orkneys and out the other side, and then sail in an arc down to Wick, safely clear of the eastern end of the Pentland Firth. The Orkneys did have difficult and strong tides but we'd had a lot of dealings with tides by now and it was all to do with getting the timing right. Our brains were hurting with the strain of major decision making so we decided we should put the idea of going round Cape Wrath on the back burner and concentrate on being in the Western Isles. Our current plan was to poke our heads out beyond the Sound of Mull and sail around the Small Isles and the Skye area. We were even considering paying a visit to the Outer Hebrides. The weather was still sublime and we were keen to prolong the opportunity to see as much of Scotland's amazing west coast archipelago while the sun was still shining.

Tobermory is tucked into the north-east corner of the Isle of Skye and is only a short sail away from Oban along the Sound of Mull. It was originally founded in 1788 as a fishing port and is the capital of the Isle of Mull as well as a burgh. A burgh is an autonomous corporate entity – something that is only found in Scotland and the north of England – but the title now has little more than ceremonial value.

Tobermory turned out to be everything I'd expected with its brightly painted houses and harbour full of bobbing boats. It's so seriously quaint and attractive that it's often chosen as the location for television and film productions like the children's show *Ballamory*. You can buy souvenirs connected to the various productions in many of the shops.

Tobermory is inevitably a magnet for tourists but it's also a working town with its still thriving fishing industry and whisky distillery. Fishing here now includes ecologically more sound practices, such as diving for scallops, which saves ravaging the seabed by trawling and turning it into an aquatic wasteland. It was lovely at the time we were there but I don't think we would have liked it at the height of summer. From our mooring buoy in the harbour, we were able to admire Tobermory from a distance. We decided that it had to be one of the prettiest seaside towns in Scotland.

We were torn between spending a whole day on the Isle of Mull or sailing out to the Small Isles. We finally chose to sail because it was a unique opportunity to go to places we wouldn't otherwise be likely to visit. The Small Isles is the name given to a tiny group of – guess what – small islands. The main isles are Canna, Rum, Eigg and Muck, and, with names like that, were begging to be visited. Having read that tiny Canna was a particularly special isle with white sandy beaches and turquoise sea we thought we would see that one first and anchor overnight. We might even have a swim!

Canna

The Isle of Canna is a remote little island measuring only 4.3 three miles long and 1.5 miles wide. There is a lack of basic facilities like a shop or daily means of transport, but the National Trust of Scotland, who manage the island, were in the process of developing and supporting the existing community while endeavouring to preserve the island's natural beauty. The isle was gifted to the National Trust of Scotland by a well-known Gaelic scholar, the late Sir John Lorne Campbell, a man whose life's work was all about conservation. At the time we were there, Canna only had twelve human inhabitants and, we discovered later, an estimated sixteen thousand rabbits. That works out at more than a thousand rabbits per head of population and on Canna the rabbit issue had clearly become a contentious one.

The list of rabbit misdemeanours included causing a major landslide, which destroyed the main road (admittedly, we're not talking the A46), digging up graves and dragging the bones out, causing walls to fall down and generally wreaking havoc within the tiny island community with their incessant burrowing. The rabbit population had exploded since the island had rid itself of its rat problem. Unfortunately, this also resulted in removing the rabbit's natural predators; they unwittingly exchanged one problem for another. With few predators left (the local birds of prey weren't effective enough by themselves), the unhampered rabbits naturally got stuck into reproducing in the way that only rabbits can. The only solution was to get a specialist rabbit exterminator in and, in fact, this idea was in the pipeline, along with many of the rabbits by the sound of it.

We anchored *Bella Rosa* in an enclosed and very sheltered cove opposite a few tiny houses and the tiniest restaurant we'd ever come across. The restaurant only opened at times when they managed to have food available to cook. I wondered if rabbit stew was a staple on the menu. We took the dinghy ashore to look around the island, and immediately met one of Canna's newest inhabitants, a young woman, whose husband had recently been appointed head gardener at Canna House. They'd moved to Canna from Suffolk, and I couldn't help thinking that it must be quite a culture shock for them, even coming from somewhere as rural as that. She told us that she and her husband both enjoyed photographing wildlife, which was a stroke of luck because appreciating wildlife was pretty much it on the list of ways to entertain yourself on Canna. Breeding, of course, was also a highly popular pursuit if the rabbits were anything to go by.

A ferry came to Canna three times a week with supplies, and unless, like us, you came in your own boat, that was also the only means of getting on and off the island. With the strong tides that swirled around the islands, swimming was definitely not an option, despite the proximity of Rum, Canna's nearest neighbour. It must have felt strange to live in a place with such limited opportunities to escape and only eleven other people to talk to, but then there would always be a regular influx of visitors to offer some light relief.

The 10.00 a.m. Saturday ferry arrived with quite a number of people on board. We found ourselves willing them all to stay put to make a change from us being the sole visitors. Bob had his binoculars trained on the ferry's gangway and counted seven people (one with a bike) and a dog preparing to disembark. Some of them had luggage and looked like they were planning on staying. We'd read that there were several self-catering cottages and a guest house on Canna, so visitors were well catered for.

The existence of Canna House was a big surprise to us. The house is a large, detached manse, a stone's throw from the water's edge. We discovered that there was a once-a-week guided tour around the house and the gardens and, luckily for us, there was a tour planned on the day we were there. The Campbell's main interest was Gaelic music, and John Campbell had collected a huge archive of traditional Gaelic folk songs and stories. The library contained the world's largest collection of Gaelic literature. Without the Campbell's efforts and commitment, much of Scotland's Gaelic heritage could have been lost or remained unavailable. Here, it was available for all to see, and kept safe all in one place for the interest and education of generations to come. There was far more to the island of Canna than first met the eye.

It was a good decision to spend a whole day on Canna. We named it as one of our best days to date. After an enthralling tour of Canna House, we spent the rest of the day walking and reading, and we even went for a swim, with me wearing my industrial strength wetsuit and Bob braving the 15 degrees C in just a pair of trunks! We ended a perfect day with a visit to the tiny restaurant, which was run by a Dutchman called Aart and his Scottish born wife, Amanda. Aart was also the island's coastguard. The food was superb, and we were unexpectedly entertained by one of the other guests playing his guitar. We sat outside having a singsong until the light began to fade. A day couldn't get a lot better than our day on Canna.

Canna to East Loch Tarbert on South Harris in the Outer Hebrides

It was quite a wrench leaving the unique and charismatic Canna, but we were being lured by the even more exciting prospect of sailing to the group of islands called the Outer Hebrides, located due west of us. The Outer Hebrides comprise a long line of compact islands that pretty much form the outer limit of the Western Isles of Scotland. They act as a breakwater for the great mass of the North Atlantic Sea. Our aim was to sail to East Loch Tarbert, a small fishing port on South Harris. To get there, we had to cross a stretch of sea called the Little Minch. The cute and endearing name belies its reputation as a wild and dangerous beast of a sea – and it wasn't little either. Our personal experience of the Little Minch was that it was a vast, dormant and empty stretch of unbelievably tranquil water. With no other vessels in sight, and not a trace of wind, it was as flat and as reflective as a mirror. It was hard to imagine it being any different but we knew how fickle the sea can be and how easily and quickly it might rise up and become a hostile force.

We were now in unimagined territory and had ventured significantly beyond what we thought we would be doing and what we thought we'd have the courage to do. The Outer Hebrides are very much 'out', and their remoteness instilled in us a whole range of emotions from feelings of excitement and adventure to vulnerability and trepidation. There was a palpable sense of being on the edge of Europe.

Travelling so far from the safer haven of the coast of mainland Scotland was a bold move, but the weather promised to stay calm, and it was the perfect opportunity for us to see the outer reaches of western Scotland before scuttling for cover again. The regular weather, safety and navigation broadcasts from the nearby Stornoway coastguard station, stationed at the north-east corner of the Outer Hebrides, helped to foster the sense of romance and remoteness of our new destination while at the same time bolstering our levels of confidence that assistance was at hand if we needed it.

The journey to East Loch Tarbert took more than seven hours and, despite the fact that it was a normal-looking small town with an occasional ferry to the mainland, we still had a strong sense of being a long way from civilisation as we knew it. It was too difficult to moor near the town itself so we anchored in a nearby secluded cove and stayed on the boat for the evening with the intention of visiting the town of East Loch Tarbert the following day.

That night, the wind unexpectedly started to strengthen and the weather began to change for the worse. We were in for an anxious night on anchor, trapped in the middle of nowhere, on what felt like the edge of the world.

Out in the Outer Hebrides

At 3.30 a.m., we were woken because the wind was howling loudly and gusting up to 30 knots, and poor *Bella Rosa* was bucking in the water like a trainee rodeo horse. This onset of strong winds had not been forecast but it looked worryingly like normal British sailing conditions had resumed! Our general fear was that, as we had no choice but to stay put on anchor for a prolonged period, the extra pressure on the anchor chain might cause the anchor to drag. If that were to happen, we were in danger of ending up being pulverised on the nearby rocky shore.

I put a position and track mark on the chart plotter to show our existing position and in order to see whether we moved significantly away from that spot. Some movement would naturally be expected as the wind shifted its direction and caused us to swing around a bit. The chart plotter showed a mass of thin, black, squiggly lines that had plotted where we had been, but, fortunately, we never moved very far from our original position and the rocks remained at a safe distance. It would have been hard to sleep soundly in those conditions so we decided that throughout the night we would take turns on deck to keep a look out, and I was first up.

In northern Scotland, during the midsummer weeks, it never really gets completely dark. The night was warm and the rocks and hills surrounding us were well defined against the pale, grey sky. The comfort of the warm night air helped soften any lurking anxiety, but I knew that this was purely psychological and had no bearing on the potentially dangerous effects of a strong wind. Over the hills to the west, a pale orange glow began to span the sky and, between the loud slapping noises of the water against the boat and the intermittent gusting sounds of the wind, the morning chorus of birdsong began to fill the air. Despite the adverse conditions, I found myself loving being up on deck by myself in the early hours of the morning, watching the glorious sunrise from the wild waters of the Outer Hebrides.

Even though I was bizarrely enjoying my night session in the cockpit, I was looking forward to getting back to the predictability of mooring buoys and pontoons. Being the first time on our trip around Britain that we'd anchored overnight, we only just discovered that our anchor light wasn't working. This seemed like a good argument for not anchoring overnight ever again because I certainly wasn't going to be shinning up the mast to fix it, and Bob wasn't going to be allowed to. At 5.30 a.m., when it came to Bob's turn to be on deck, he annoyingly said, "Ach, it'll be alreet" in a bad imitation of a Scottish accent and rolled over and went back to sleep. What a con! In future, if we were ever to be in this position again, he would have to do the first watch while I stayed in bed.

After breakfast on our still very rocky boat, we discussed the idea that we might be sitting in a 'wind acceleration zone', which is an area at the base of high or mountainous ground. It seemed plausible because that was the nature of the area where we were anchored and the inshore forecast hadn't predicted these winds. In these zones, the wind rushes down the slope, building up speed as it goes, thus subjecting the area at the base of the high ground to much stronger winds than the average at the time. In our case, we could have been sitting in a whirl of 30 knots of wind while the rest of Scotland was enjoying a pleasant 10 knots.

While, in truth, it didn't really seem likely, we talked ourselves into it in order to gear ourselves up for the trip back to mainland Scotland. If we didn't make a move, would we be marooned with steadily diminishing supplies of cans of curry and dried pasta? At least we had the phone and good radio contact, so we rang the Stornoway coastguard for a local weather forecast and some advice. As it turned out, members of the coastguard are not allowed to give sailors advice but can only give us the Met Office forecast and leave it to you to make the decision whether to stay or whether to go. The current forecast was for a north-easterly Force 6 and, despite Bob trying every trick in the book to get them to speak 'off the record' and tell us what to do, all they would say was that "The Little Minch can develop big seas in north-easterlies". I suppose that was a pretty pointed comment.

By now, we were aching to leave the Outer Hebrides and get back to safe territory, but I was reluctant to submit ourselves to six to eight hours of beating against a strong north-east wind. After much deliberation, we finally agreed that we would up anchor and go out a little way to see if it was as bad as the Stornoway coastguard had suggested. If it was bad out there, we would just turn round and come back. As we left the cove and entered the main channel leading to East Loch Tarbert, the swell on our port beam increased and the gusts were still in excess of 30 knots. Very quickly, we could see that the passage across the Little Minch would be too long, too arduous and very likely a bit dangerous, so we agreed that we should turn back. At that moment, the Stornoway coastguard answered a May Day call, which put the wind up us even more – so to speak – and served to confirm that we'd probably made the right decision. Back in our cove, we had a few unsuccessful attempts at anchoring, but eventually got a good hold, and although we were still swinging around in gusts of 25 knots we now regarded the cove as a wonderfully safe haven after all. It's all relative.

One of our biggest regrets was that we never managed to set foot on Harris. It was too risky to leave *Bella Rosa* on anchor on her own, and the short journey by dinghy to the shore would have been too choppy for a small inflatable boat. The risk of capsizing was too great. I imagined that we weren't missing much, given the weather, but I would have liked to have bought something in genuine Harris Tweed, even if it was just a hat. We vowed to return one day, but in a civilised manner, by ferry, with someone else at the helm.

Maybe it was our Outer Hebrides experience that caused us both to reconsider the idea of going round Cape Wrath. The strong tides and dangerous overfalls around the Pentland Firth, and even through the Orkneys, were once again beginning to sound a bit too challenging. The benign weather up to this point had lulled us into a false sense of security. We were also conscious that if we were to go round the top we would have to get a move on and would have to miss out on seeing many other stunning cruising areas like the Summer Isles. The more northern part of Scotland was said to be bleak and featureless compared to the verdant mountainous area we were in. There were also some good restaurants that shouldn't be missed!

By the evening of the second day on anchor, the Stornoway coastguard was predicting the winds to die down to a more manageable Force 5 later (within twelve hours), and we decided that the following day was when we would make our move back across the Little Minch to the mainland, where we would have time to reflect on what to do next.

Nowhere to Park in Loch Torridon

The winds finally did die down as predicted, and at last we were going to be able to cross back to the Inner Hebrides. Typically, an early morning start was necessary to get the benefits of a fair tide, and we finally left our cove at 6.15 in the morning. Sailing out into the glowing morning light, we could feel that the air had become much chillier and we resorted to piling on multiple layers of thermals again. Our day was destined to be uneventful but we were looking forward to what promised to be a pleasant sail on a beam reach back to good old mainland Scotland.

At first, the Little Minch, which is the size of Manchester (but without the buildings), was completely empty of other vessels. Even on our journey to Harris we'd only seen one fishing boat, and that was miles in the distance. Risk of collision was a constant companion in the busy Solent, our home sailing area, but our natural assumption in the Little Minch was that it would never be an issue. In any case, it was a bright, clear day and we could see for miles. It was quite a surprise, then, to see that there was another yacht on the far horizon that appeared to be heading across our own heading. We were under sail and could see that the other boat was motoring. Given that the rules of the road state that power gives way to sail, we naturally expected that if we did get close to each other the other boat would make their intentions clear in plenty of time, as they were obliged to do, and allow us to continue on our course unimpeded.

We watched the other yacht with interest until it

became very clear that we were on a collision course, and still no action was being taken. As the stand-on boat, our job was to hold our course for as long as was viable and wait for the other boat to take clear avoiding action. Our nerves were being tested, but we continued on our course, thinking that they were merely taking their time. Up to this point, we couldn't make out anyone on the helm, but by now we were close enough to see that the boat was a Hallberg Rassy 54 and bearing a Danish ensign. Eventually, a woman appeared on deck, so we both started bellowing loudly in her direction to try to catch her attention in case she hadn't seen us. She waved back in a jolly and enthusiastic fashion, and was grinning like a Cheshire cat, but still didn't change course. Was she coming over to compare notes about the merits of owning a Hallberg Rassy? Time was running out fast, and we were beginning to suspect that we may have come across an escaped lunatic, who'd stolen a boat and was out to attack anyone within striking distance. I checked to see if she had any machine guns trained on us. At the last minute, we were forced to take control of the situation ourselves, and bore away ninety degrees to starboard, missing being carved up by the still smiling Danish woman by mere seconds.

Completely unnerved by the situation, we were both now hurling a stream of verbal abuse after her as she motored off into the sunrise. Bob's line of enquiry at full volume was why was she in charge of a boat at all, but she continued to smile inanely in our direction. I could see that her boat was called *Cecilia*, so Bob was able to grab the radio and call her directly. He was surprisingly polite when he suggested that she learn the rules of the road properly in future to avoid nearly killing anyone else. She repeatedly said she was sorry and promised to be more careful in future. We couldn't quite believe what had happened and spent the next couple of hours in stunned silence, munching our way through the chocolate and biscuit supplies, hoping it would help neutralise the shock.

The dramatic Loch Torridon was our chosen destination, and our intention was to leave our boat on a mooring buoy owned by one of the lochside hotels and spend a civilised night in the hotel. It seemed like an excellent plan in theory but, in reality, the mooring buoy mentioned in the guidebook no longer existed and anchoring was not feasible. What's more, the hotel looked like it was holding a Hells Angels convention. We were still feeling fairly wrung out, but it seemed like we had no choice but to move on. We hadn't wanted another night on anchor anyway. By now, we'd been on *Bella Rosa* without getting off for three whole days and were desperate to find somewhere we could leave her safely and securely. We carried on reluctantly for four more hours to beautiful Plockton, where we were able to find a more reliable visitor buoy and go ashore.

Plockton

After seventy-two hours of rocking and rolling on *Bella Rosa*, the first fifteen minutes of attempting to walk to the centre of Plockton felt like walking on a gigantic air bed. We'd woken up to fabulous weather and were going to have a whole day off to acclimatise to normal cruising life again, see if our legs remembered their main purpose and have a rest from worrying about being shipwrecked. Our circular walk took us past Duncraig Castle, an imposing, castle-like house that was being refurbished as a guest house. It looked like a miniature Hogwarts and would make an amazing venue for a big party.

Plockton was where we encountered the notorious Scottish midge for the first time. They were just coming out of hibernation ready for a long, juicy summer gorging on human blood.

We were so glad that we came across the lovely village of Plockton. It's a tiny Narnia of a place in a *Lord of the Rings* setting, with toy-town cottages and exquisite little well-tended gardens fronting on to the harbour. The abundance of palm trees gave it a very continental feel, and I couldn't think of anywhere else quite like it on the British coast. At the time of our visit, Plockton had a few shops, two hotels, a pub and, above all, ten sturdy mooring buoys for visiting yachties like ourselves. What more could you ask for when you've just braved a precarious few days on anchor on the edge of a remote rocky outcrop?

The Plockton Hotel, which is also a thriving pub, was hosting a Scottish music night, so our entertainment for the evening was sorted. I was surprised at the large number of foreign tourists coming into the pub. There were several groups of suave Italians and young Americans all eating there, along with some retired northern Europeans that you always find in Scotland in May. I noted how much more stylish the Italians manage to look in the same stuff that we all wear in the UK – jeans, T-shirts and maybe a casually draped scarf. I spent the whole of lunch trying to work out what their secret ingredient was but could only conclude that it was youth, poise and uber trendy glasses. I made a mental note to visit the opticians as soon as I got home.

At the Scottish music night, we found ourselves sitting next to Jo and David, who, we discovered, were also going round Britain on *Dawn Treader*, a Hallberg Rassy. They'd set off from Dartmouth on 5 May and, annoyingly, had managed to avoid some of the bad weather that we'd experienced. We discovered that they were doing the full circumnavigation via Cape Wrath to the Orkneys. This completely unsettled us again into thinking that maybe we should after all gird our loins, or something similar, and do the same. As Jo said, it's not really going round Britain if you don't go over the top! All of this continual agonising over which route to take was beginning to put us in a permanent state of anxiety so we decided that, while all options were still open, any more thinking about the decision would be put on hold for now and we'd just enjoy being in the Western Isles.

Plockton to the Kyle of Lochalsh

The Kyle of Lochalsh is only an hour and a half away from Plockton by boat, and involves sailing under the relatively new Skye road bridge, which at its centre point sits at twenty-nine metres above the highest astronomical tide. Our air draft, which is the measurement from the top of our mast to the waterline, is only sixteen metres, but knowing that we should have plenty of clearance room still didn't stop us from holding our breath and ducking when we passed under the bridge!

The facilities in the Kyle of Lochalsh are limited but there is a good, solid, wooden pontoon available for visiting boat people, and a great Co-op. The Lochalsh Co-op has to be in one of the best supermarket locations in the whole of the British Isles with its spectacular, unbroken panoramic ocean and mountain views. I never thought I'd get excited about visiting a Co-op, but we hadn't been able to stock up on good-quality fresh food since being in Tobermory a week previously, and the thought of seeing an abundance of bright green lettuces and glossy red tomatoes was almost overwhelming.

Later in the day, a very distinguished-looking, eighty-foot Oyster sailing yacht arrived, with the word 'Gordonstoun' splashed in large white lettering across its sail cover. It hovered around elegantly before sliding over to the pontoon to moor next to us. As the name suggested, the yacht was in fact the property of the famous Gordonstoun School, and was a yacht with attitude. We'd both clearly attended the wrong schools. Given that Gordonstoun's alumni include both the Duke of Edinburgh and Prince Charles, and that the two life rafts alone were the size of two massive whisky barrels, we knew that we were about to fraternise with the grandest of British grand.

Despite there being at least twenty strapping young men on board, they unhesitatingly accepted Bob's offer to help them tie up. Perhaps they were so used to being waited on that they assumed Bob had been stationed there purely to serve. I have to confess that I frequently tried to enforce the same conditions on our boat but not always with as much success. I lurked warily behind the spray hood to watch with interest how a boat that size would cope with the mooring but, with Bob's expert assistance, they did a decent enough job.

On closer scrutiny, I was very puzzled by the general appearance of the crew. I was expecting foppish hairdos and the assured gestures of the upper echelons of British aristocratic society, but this crew were tattooed and earringed, and had a rough, tough demeanour about them. Had Gordonstoun become more liberal with its choice of pupils? It all fell reassuringly into place when we discovered that Gordonstoun sometimes loans out their boat and that the young men were in fact soldiers from the Scottish Black Watch regiment. We still felt compelled to bow slightly in deference each time we walked past.

The Kyle of Lochalsh to Inverie

The Kyle Rhea is roughly a two-mile-long narrow channel between the Isle of Skye and the mainland, and most of it is only about 0.2 miles wide. When the tide squeezes itself into the narrow channel from the open sea, it can run very fast and can throw up some unpredictable currents and whirlpools. Once again, the timing of a passage is crucial and we needed to set off by 6 o'clock in the morning to catch the strong, south-going tide.

Whirlpools can be very dangerous, like the one in the Gulf of Corryvreckan, but any whirlpools in the Kyle Rhea would be tame by comparison and fascinating to sail through provided that they didn't cause us to lose our steering and throw us off course. We were both excited and nervous about the prospect of surfing through the Kyle Rhea.

Even though our timing was spot on, the water was creating all sorts of strange patterns and we were being swept along at nearly 11 knots at one stage and not always in a straight line. It was nature's idea of a theme park, and turned out to be thoroughly enjoyable and fun without being dangerous. To cap it all, we were surrounded by mountains and glorious scenery.

Towards the end of the Kyle Rhea, we turned east into Loch Nevis to visit a village called Inverie, the only village on the Knoydart Peninsula. Knoydart was bought out by its residents in 1997 and, to its inhabitants, community is all important. Inverie's overriding charm is that it is only accessible by sea, or via an eighteen-mile hike over rough terrain and a series of Munros. There are no roads leading to it or from it. There are, however, a few roads in Inverie itself, and some of the locals own cars.

Sad to say, our initial welcome was not a very friendly one when we dinghied ashore with a black bin bag of rubbish from our boat. A passing local shouted at us fairly aggressively that we were forbidden to bring our rubbish ashore because they had to pay for their own rubbish removal. We hadn't seen any sign to that effect until he pointed to it, but on the other side of the jetty from the side we had come in. We fully understood the problem, but he could have asked us politely!

We left the bag on the dinghy and scuttled off to take refuge in a quirky café run by a couple of local girls. The café had allegedly been designated by someone or other of note as being one of the top fifteen cafés in the world. It was an attractive café but, although the coffee was good and the view over the bay stunning, my personal top fifteen cafés were still pretty much all in Ireland. I could only imagine that whoever had made that bold statement had just arrived exhausted after an eighteen-mile hike in bad weather and was so desperate for sanctuary that even a McDonalds would have come close to the top of their list.

A man at a nearby table did talk to us, but it was more of a subtle interrogation than a friendly chat. Uneasy thoughts of paganism and the film *The Wicker Man* started to invade my mind. These initial lightly suspicious thoughts naturally led to worst case scenario thoughts like should we carry one of *Bella Rosa*'s fire extinguishers around in our backpacks in case we ended up as live sacrifices on a burning pyre? They would have to be desperate to bother to offer up a couple of old English fogeys like us to appease any residing deities. However, with the community's obvious limited access to virgins – or even chickens – we felt it was wise to remain on our guard.

The Inverie community is about one hundred and twenty strong but seems to have attracted people from all over the world to settle there. At first, as well as being met with hostile suspicion, we sensed a smug self-righteousness among the residents. This attitude seemed to ease off a bit when everyone got stuck into the booze at the Old Forge Restaurant. There was – weirdly, we subsequently discovered – a very strong Australian presence, and most of the holidaymakers and visitors we spoke to were from far afield. It was all about escaping from normal, frenetic life and creating their own small paradise, or maybe running from something – literally or metaphorically. The Old Forge is dubbed the remotest pub in mainland Britain, and was being run by an Aussie with a big personality, which partially explained why there were so many other Aussies in Inverie. He must have invited all his mates and relatives for a prolonged visit!

The pub walls were strewn with a variety of musical instruments, ancient and modern, and patrons were encouraged to play them if they were so inclined. Luckily for the other diners, neither Bob nor myself was tempted to have a go as we were far too intent on trying to enjoy our dinner while keeping an eye on everyone else in the pub to make sure they weren't about to tie us up and offer us to the pagan god of fertility, although, in my case, it was more likely to be the pagan god of post-menopause, if there is one.

We survived our intense visit to Inverie and hastened back to the security of *Bella Rosa*. We weren't at all sorry that we'd visited but were a little confused by the strange atmosphere of the place. It was almost as if many of them were trying to put on a show of living the Utopian dream but underneath they knew it wasn't delivering. They were cut off from reality, and life was very limited in many respects. Those who thought that living in such a tight-knit, remote community would solve all their worldly problems had been left with nothing and no one else to blame but themselves for not finding happiness and fulfilment. We'd like to go back again one day and hopefully disabuse ourselves of these mildly negative impressions. Hopefully, it was just a coincidence that a lot of people were having a bad day!

Back to Tobermory Again

Enough of pagan Britain! We couldn't wait to get back to civilisation so we spent a delightful day sailing past the east coast of Eigg into the Sound of Mull, heading back to Tobermory with its brightly painted houses, whisky distillery and its reassuringly accessible range of transport and roads. The Diamond Jubilee was imminent but, so far, when we asked anyone if there were likely to be any celebrations in Scotland, they just shrugged disinterestedly. We figured that if anywhere in the vicinity was celebrating in style it would be Tobermory.

Tobermory was truly abuzz with boat life. There were five times as many boats as there had been when we passed through more than a week previously. Quite a number of yachts had Union Jack bunting flying and some other boats were 'dressed overall', which in boat-speak is sporting a string of international signal flags running from the bow to the stern via the masthead. Apparently, there is a specific sequence of flags that must be followed, each of which spells out a letter or message. Offensive or indecent messages in any language are not permissible. It would be time-consuming and tedious work to monitor flag flying, and it would take a multi-lingual signal flag expert with time on his hands to spot which of the boats was saying 'b***er off, you landlubber b****rds' in English, let alone Punjabi or Yoruba.

Wanting to join in with the spirit of things, I'd bought some bunting in a chandlery back in Oban. I assumed it was in accordance with the international signal flag code and I hadn't picked up the one saying 'Happy 90th Birthday, Grandma'. It was only when I had it strung out on deck that I realised that I didn't know how to get it to the top of the mast without leaving the safety of the deck. After much brainstorming over the possibilities, we had to settle for it being strung round the guard rail at thigh level, which wasn't anywhere near as satisfying but was better than nothing. We surveyed the jolly scene and anticipated an impromptu outdoor party later that evening. Who would be first to get the ball rolling?

The boating fraternity were now looking more like we had expected them to look. When we first set off on 16th April, the other sailors we came across were mainly solitary men with unkempt beards and holey sweaters. After a few weeks, we progressed to meeting the occasional boatload of men and pairs of men of all ages with varying reasons to be out on the water. We'd met the boatload of chaps who had been competing in the Three Peaks challenge, we'd met George and John, who were sailing together because their wives weren't interested in sailing, and then, eventually, we met Jo and David, who were sailing round Britain like we were. We didn't come across our first 'normal' couple until we were halfway up the east coast of Ireland.

In Tobermory, there were still quite a few 'men-only' boats, and various men were frequently to be seen pacing up and down the pontoons, smoking cigarettes and with mobile phones glued to their ears. A typical conversation being, "Yes, darling, we're having a very nice time, thank you, but it would have been nicer if you'd been here. I'm sorry you're having to deal with our five children over this bank holiday all by yourself... I'll call you again tomorrow. Bye for now." Then there'd be the phhhizzzz sound of a can of beer opening.

There were many family-crewed yachts out as well, one or two with salty sea dogs on board, sporting neat little doggy life jackets. West Highland terriers seemed to be the favourite dog breed, but then we were in the western Highlands. Many of the children were busy with little fishing nets or were being allowed to row around in dinghies unsupervised. There were some impressive-looking ensigns flying from the back of many of the yachts. Our ensign was the very common red flag with the Union Jack in the corner but some of them were clearly special and denoted membership of exclusive sailing clubs or senior ranking of some kind. We were pleased with our sailing achievements to date and thought we deserved a special ensign denoting our ability to make it so far while keeping the boat the right way up. Our top-quality Union Jack tea towel would have made an unusual and thought-provoking ensign, but people might have thought we were seasoned sailors and come to us for advice, so we didn't attach it.

A Day in Tobermory

Nothing! No party. No Jubilee celebration. The bunting had given us a totally false impression. Maybe we were in nationalist and republican territory! We did the laundry, walked to a lighthouse and then went to a restaurant for steak and chips instead. At least it wasn't raining, and the midges were out in only modest numbers.

Tobermory to Oban

We had to tear ourselves away from Tobermory. It was so seductive with its brightly coloured harbourside buildings, friendly and protected harbour, numerous cafés and delightful shops and, above all, the modern marina with top-quality facilities. We needed to go back to Oban to collect our post from the marina office but it wasn't that far to go and would only take a few hours. It was a spring tide, so we did a bit of 'punching the tide' to get down the Sound of Mull and to squeeze ourselves through the southern neck of it. The tide was also squeezing itself through and produced one of the most interesting overfall effects that we'd seen. It looked like the water was boiling furiously, but with white foaming crests instead of steam. We knew our engine was powerful enough to push our way through but, even so, we were reduced to doing only one and a half knots for a short while. At least we didn't start going backwards, but then we did love Tobermory.

Due to past experiences, we had now adopted a 'guilty until proved innocent' stance with any other boats that came within a three-mile radius and found ourselves on 'red alert' most of the time we were out on the water. It did heighten our awareness of what we were doing even more than it had been, but luckily didn't detract from our enjoyment.

During our trip down the Sound of Mull, we became concerned that our depth gauge wasn't working properly. Ninety per cent of the time it was absolutely fine but, all of a sudden, the depth gauge would tell us that we only had a few metres under the keel, and this went on for several minutes. This happened repeatedly and, even though I knew from the charts that we were in a deep water area and knew that this was impossible, it did freak us out a bit. We had been told that with Scotland housing an important British naval base and submarine practice area they sometimes use passing yachts as tracking practice. This could have explained everything, unless the Loch Ness monster was having an away day or a mini-break in the Sound of Mull.

Oban to Mallaig

If anyone had been looking at our recent water track, they would have thought we'd lost the plot around the Skye and Mull area or were searching for something we'd accidentally dropped overboard. We'd said we were reluctant to leave Tobermory, so, after leaving Oban (which was a very short visit this time), we decided to go past it yet again and wave furiously at it. We liked the area so much that we didn't want to leave – especially with the local weather being so sunny and fresh – but, for a change, I decided that we'd head out of the northern end of the Sound of Mull to Mallaig that night and, for the Admirable Bob's birthday the following day, we'd go to Portree. As Bob didn't appear to be that fussed about how he was going to spend his birthday, I planned to surprise him with a day's ... sailing! It could be the start of something!

Mallaig is an authentic and thriving fishing town, which reminded us of Newlyn. It was buzzing with activity when we arrived, and there was something quite exciting about sharing moorings with numerous large fishing vessels and their industrious crews. It's such a tough job, and we could only feel great admiration and respect for those men who tolerate extreme weather conditions and personal danger for often only a meagre living. Mallaig was a good place for us to stock up on provisions in the large local Co-op. There was something about the name Mallaig that made me want to keep saying it out loud and linger on the 'laig' part.

Mallaig to Portree

In Portree, we hoped to find somewhere extra special for a romantic dinner. The birthday present situation was a little tricky because I'd had limited opportunity to find anything interesting. I'd collected a few things along the way, but they didn't amount to much more than some stripey sailor socks and a T-shirt with the world 'ocean' on it. He was lucky that it wasn't just a packet of shortbread, a tattoo voucher from Milford Haven and a lucky shamrock from Ireland. We spent most of the day getting from Mallaig to Portree, and it wasn't the most exciting birthday Bob had ever had, but it was different and I had prepared a nice salad for lunch on the hoof.

We went in search of a nice restaurant for the birthday dinner but, despite the fact that it was midweek and Portree was just a small Scottish Highland town, all the good restaurants were fully booked. What was going on, we asked ourselves? Luckily, the cleverly-disguised-so-that-no-one-knew-it-was-a- restaurant Café Arriba did eventually manage to squeeze us in for a Mexican-style salmon steak and a glass of vino verde. Local atmosphere and produce – you can't beat it! Bob was happy enough because he'd had lots of birthday greetings from family and friends via email, blog, text, card and carrier seagull. He was also quite touched by the poem about Portree that his brother Terry sent him.

Lines Penned at Euston
(By One Who is Not Going)

By A M HARBOARD

Stranger with the pile of luggage proudly labelled for Portree,
How I wish this night of August I were you and you were me!
Think of all that lies before you when the train goes sliding forth
And the lines athwart the sunset lead you swiftly to the North!
Think of breakfast at Kingussie, think of high Drumochter Pass,
Think of highland breezes singing through the bracken and the grass.
Scabious blue and yellow daisy, tender fern beside the train,
Rowdy tummel falling, brawling, seen and lost and glimpsed again!
You will pass my golden roadway of the days of long ago.
Will you realise the magic of the names I used to know:
Clachnaharry, Achnashellash, Achnasheen and Duirinish?
Ev'ry moor alive with coveys, every pool aboil with fish;
Every well-remembered vista more exciting by the mile,
Till the wheeling gulls are screaming round the engine at the Kyle.
Think of cloud on Bheinn na Cailleach, jagged Cuillins soaring high,
Scent of peat and all the glamour of the misty Isle of Skye!
Rods and gun case in the carriage, wise retriever in the van,
Go, and good luck travel with you!
(Wish I'd half your luck, my man!)

Portree to Lochinver
(And a Day Off in Lochinver)

We made the momentous decision to carry on to Lochinver, which indicated that our idea of sailing round the top of Scotland was no longer just a frivolous fantasy but was becoming a serious reality. Having got that far, we knew the chances of us backing out were as slim as me saying no to a glass of champagne on my birthday. We were on a mission to circumnavigate mainland Britain in an authentic and proper way. Chopping off the top of Scotland by going via the Caledonian was now never going to be satisfying enough, and the thought of tackling Neptune's Staircase, a series of eight consecutive locks along the Caledonian, made the prospect of going round Cape Wrath almost seem like taking the easy option. For us relatively novice sailors, it was still going to be a tough call, both mentally and physically. Getting over to the Orkneys successfully from Kinlochbervie would be our very own version of getting to the summit of Everest. We were becoming steadily braced for the challenge, and it was a thrilling sensation.

After a heavy night making birthday whoopee at the Arriba in Portree, we were in bed by 9.30 p.m. ready to be up at 5.00 a.m. to catch the north-going tide towards Lochinver. The next morning, we emerged on deck to face a stunningly beautiful dawn. There was still a luminous, creamy moon hanging in the rusty orange sky, and the sea was calm and glass-like. It was hard to imagine that such a benign scene could ever turn nasty, but strong winds were forecast later that evening and we wanted to be tucked up safely in Lochinver well before the weather changed.

Lochinver is only thirty miles south of Cape Wrath, and beyond that is Kinlochbervie, which is only fifteen miles further on. After Lochinver, we'd scheduled one final overnight stop at Kinlochbervie to allow us time to gather our courage and finely tune our nerves before embarking on our intrepid fourteen-hour sail to the Orkney Islands.

The Islands of the Outer Hebrides to the west of us provided a certain amount of protection from the Atlantic swell, but beyond the islands lay a wilder, more exposed, section of the North Sea. The north coast of Scotland and its adjacent sea is not – as I'd always previously imagined – a verdant floral paradise with tiny, wildlife-filled coves. It is hostile, barren and remote with a fearsome reputation. There are very few bolt-holes in which to take refuge if things were to turn unexpectedly nasty. The first viable bolt-hole is ten miles east of Cape Wrath and is called Loch Eribol, otherwise known as Loch Horrible, which just about sums it up. With winds from the north, even taking refuge in Loch Eribol wouldn't work. Thirty-six miles east of Loch Eribol is a small ferry port at Scrabster, which would provide better shelter, but, having got that far, the Orkneys would probably be a better option. It was also the case that, once round Cape Wrath, turning back was not an option either in an east-going tide. It was not for the faint-hearted!

Once we arrived in Lochinver, we bumped into two boats that we'd come across earlier on in the Western Isles. One was *Dawn Treader*, crewed by Jo and David, and now also joined by Graham. The other one was a Dutch barge called *Guillemot*, owned by a retired Dutchman and his English wife. They were both planning on sailing to the Orkneys. It was nice to think that we might have company, and a bit of a flotilla might be all-round jolly good fun in-between the terrifying bits!

Lochinver is a spacious and very active fishing port with one small pontoon for visiting yachts. I could see why the visitor pontoon only needed to be small as there can't be that many pleasure-seeking yacht people to be found quite so far away from the Mediterranean. Despite being so far north, there was a lot going on in Lochinver. Amazingly, there was a five-star hotel and restaurant with one Michelin star offering a seven-course gourmet taster menu. The restaurant must have been mainly a destination place for tourists because I couldn't envisage the hordes of beefy-looking international trawlermen spending their hard-earned cash on 'hand-glazed Japanese tamari gently nestling in a manuka honey reduction'. We discovered a whole raft of trawlermen (the ones who weren't indulging in haute cuisine), local families and visiting yacht people (who weren't in the Mediterranean) in the very smartly done-up seamen's mission near the harbour. The food was very wholesome, ridiculously cheap and you could even take your own wine. They should have a seaman's mission on every high street. They'd have a massive success on their hands!

We decided to have a much needed day off after three days of being constantly on the go. It was a chance to see if the legs could still do forwards and backwards as well as the more unusual positions needed on a boat. It was also an opportunity for us to visit the local RNLI office to get some local knowledge and advice about the most sensible way to tackle Cape Wrath. You can't beat local knowledge when it comes to navigation.

The winds were still quite strong and coming from the north-east, which was not particularly good news for us if it continued. Sailing into the wind all the way to the Orkneys would be exhausting. The friendly lifeboatman manning the office was eager to proffer advice as well as relate several scary stories involving huge waves and perilous rescues. It seemed that general mayhem was the norm in sea areas Hebrides and Fair Isle, which was where we were and where we would be respectively if things went according to plan. It was daunting to think that we'd be sailing across sea areas that we'd only ever heard doom-laden reports about on the shipping forecast.

The lifeboatman checked the weather forecast and looked decidedly doubtful. The current conditions with the north-easterly Force 4 winds were not ideal, he told us, and it looked like it was going to carry on like that for some time. Force 4 didn't sound too bad but, even if the winds died down, it was the residual three to four metre swell created by the strong winds to date that could still make the journey quite arduous. We noted his reaction, but still felt optimistic that things might improve over the next day or two. We decided to press on to Kinlochbervie and review the situation from there. Once in Kinlochbervie, at least we would be ready to go, if a suitable window in the weather opened up.

Disconcertingly, the powers that be in Kinlochbervie were telling the Lochinver RNLI team to discourage any other yachts from coming, as they were already jammed with yachts that had been stuck waiting to sail round the top. They said that they couldn't possibly accommodate any more for the time being. This was an unexpected blow, but we refused to be deterred and decided to go to Kinlochbervie the following morning regardless, and hope that they wouldn't turn us away. The crew of *Dawn Treader* had made the same decision to go, which increased our resolve by miles.

Lochinver to Kinlochbervie

The journey from Lochinver to Kinlochbervie gave us a flavour of what might be to come when we sailed out into the open sea. We were back in big swell, and the winds were gusty and unpredictable. Helming was once more an effort but we managed to sail for the best part of the journey, tacking our way northwards in the company of *Dawn Treader*. Kinlochbervie harbour did turn out to be fairly full of both fishing vessels and yachts, but even so we found a suitable *Bella Rosa*-sized space on a pontoon, and her new friend *Dawn Treader* rafted up against us.

Once we were installed in Kinlochbervie harbour, our plan was to leave at 6.00 a.m. the following morning to reach a point just off Cape Wrath by 10.00 a.m. in time to pick up the east-going tide that would take us much of the way to the Orkneys. We would then spend twelve hours crossing the North Sea and would be able to enter the Sound of Hoy in the Orkneys at slack water. We wouldn't be able to enter the Sound any earlier because it was a significant tidal gate and the tide out of the Sound would be against us. We would log our passage with Stornoway coastguard and let them know when we arrived. Having the local coastguard be aware of our movements was always an additional comforting security measure, and they were always happy to oblige. The coastguard provides such a valuable service.

Our policy of venturing out tentatively to check the viability of any passage we were unsure about was part of our strategy for leaving Kinlochbervie. If we didn't like what we saw, we would turn back. We'd also been advised that, in the case of going round Cape Wrath, if conditions were becoming unfavourable by the time we reached a rocky outcrop known as Bodha Roin then they would be much worse by the time we reached the Cape. If that was case, it would be inadvisable to carry on. Our good weather window was long enough for us to get to the Orkneys before the next spate of bad weather but, if it turned out to be worse than predicted, we could be stuck in Kinlochbervie for some time. Going as far as Bodha Roin was now the next stage in our rolling programme of decision making. If conditions at Bodha Roin passed the test, and we carried on, we would reach Stromness by 22.00 the following evening. That was going to be one of the most welcome arrivals in the history of our sailing escapades.

I'd always assumed that Cape Wrath hadn't been called that for nothing and that it was indeed a place of wrathfulness and rage, as one might expect on the coast of north-west Scotland. What a surprise it was then to find out that it actually means 'turning place'. If we'd known that sooner, it might have always been part of the grand plan. We decided to re-christen it 'Cape Fingers Crossed', which would just about cover everything. In the light of such a misnomer, the Cape of Good Hope should be regarded with suspicion.

We had very little time to spend in Kinlochbervie but, judging by the size of the trawlers and the lorries waiting to transport the catch to various parts of Europe, it was a serious fishing port and not much else. We double- and triple-checked our passage plan, and prepared everything we could for the next day.

Kinlochbervie
To Stromness

Aargh! Not really! It was all far too surreal to be feeling apprehensive as we drank our morning tea and prepared *Bella Rosa* for her big challenge in keeping the Tyrrell team morale up by keeping us afloat and facing the right direction. At 6.00 a.m., there were at least six boats preparing for the off, including us and *Dawn Treader*. There was no sign of *Guillemot*, so she must have stayed behind in Lochinver, and who could blame her? Taking a barge out on the open seas sounded like a suicide mission at the very least.

Three of the preparing boats turned out to be of French extraction, judging by their ensigns and the amount of shrugging and gesticulating going on among their various crews. We couldn't hear the comments, but 'merde' must have come into it quite a lot. The French presence was a little bit disconcerting, as French sailors do seem to have a notorious reputation for making unfathomable, devil-may-care decisions and for not adhering to normal procedures when in charge of boats (and cars for that matter). We once saw many French sailors in action in Cherbourg marina, which was confirmation enough.

The involvement of the French counted for very little in the way of reassurance but, looking on the bright side, what they ended up doing might make what we were about to do look impressively competent. The Admirable Bob stowed the ready-prepared lunchtime sandwiches and hearty casserole to have en route, we logged our passage with Stornoway coastguard and slipped our mooring lines to chug away slowly from the safety of Kinlochbervie's protected harbour.

There was a mild swell with 8 to 9 knots of wind as we left the harbour entrance. These would have been perfect conditions had they continued, but we suspected it would hot up a bit once we hit the North Sea. Until we reached Cape Wrath, we continued to be protected from the swell by the Outer Hebrides, and the mainland was providing some protection from the full strength of the north-east wind. Once we got beyond the corner, we would no doubt be subjected to stronger winds, an unopposed swell and, for at least six hours, wind against tide. We put our sails up and made our way north-west towards Bodha Roin to make a final judgement about whether we would continue or turn back.

When we reached Bodha Roin, the conditions remained mild, so we were happy to carry on optimistically to our point of no return, just north-west of the Cape. *Dawn Treader*, a mile or two ahead of us, was doing the same and so were two of the French boats. The third French boat had disappeared from sight and was either heading for a different destination or had sunk early in the game. We listened out for May Days. As we began to carve our turn around the Cape we could feel the building strength of the east-going tide. We pointed *Bella Rosa* in the general direction of the Orkneys, put the kettle on and prepared to enjoy the ride.

To keep up our strength to cope with the long passage ahead, we took turns in being on and off duty, took lots of rest breaks, drank copious amounts of tea and allowed ourselves lots of nice snacks. If anything can justify stuffing your face with whatever takes your fancy, a fourteen-hour sail to the Orkneys can. Throughout the journey, the wind never rose more than 15 knots and the swell stayed moderate. It all went well despite having to beat into the wind the whole time. With all the build-up of tension and the anxiety on the day, we knew we would be fairly exhausted by the time we reached Stromness.

We made such good time that we arrived near Hoy Sound an hour earlier than predicted, but too early to attempt battling the strong ebb tide. The exiting tide didn't seem to stop one of the French boats ploughing on in, but they must have been going at crawling pace. It was the perfect time for us to stop a few miles off the Sound to have our hot dinner and a rest. We put the boat into a 'hove to', which is a clever thing you do with the sails to enable the boat to sit comfortably in the water without moving very far. We had plenty of sea space and were able to relax while we waited for the ebb from the Hoy Sound to subside. *Dawn Treader* must have seen us stop and kindly radioed to see if everything was alright, which was very supportive of them. They liked our dinner plans and decided to do the same thing. So, there we both were, bobbing about on the water about half a mile apart, eating our dinner in the middle of the North Sea, not yet daring to feel too self-satisfied until we were completely home and dry in Stromness marina.

Our final hour getting to Stromness was an easy one. It was ten o'clock in the evening, misty and grey when we arrived, but we'd reached the most northerly point of the whole journey to date and were thrilled with what we'd achieved. A sigh of relief was in order and it was time to have a few days off to recover our sanity and have a good look round the islands.

The Orkneys

One of the good things about going everywhere by boat was not having a car. Not having a car meant that we were forced to live our life within our immediate vicinity, which was refreshing and uncomplicated unless we were prepared to take a bus somewhere. Generally, what was on our doorstep would have to provide for all of our needs, although our needs were mostly limited to buying and eating food. If we'd needed specialist root canal treatment, or fancied a Bikram yoga session, it might have been more problematic.

The local shops in the smaller towns of the Highlands and the islands often seemed quite limited with what they had to offer, but less did frequently turn out to be more. I discovered that it was possible to survive without green beans from Kenya, ten varieties of lettuce and award-winning organic muesli, and that it's surprising what can be done with a Golden Delicious and a bendy carrot or two. The pubs and restaurants we visited all had to be within staggering distance of the boat and in normal circumstances we would probably give many of them a wide berth. Being forced to 'make do' meant we discovered hostelries that were oozing with local character and individuals we were never likely to come across in our normal lives.

There was a quiet whisper of history and heritage coming out of every pore in every place we had visited so far, and cultural and educational centres were to be found in the most unlikely places. As for social life, we met so many lovely locals who were curious about us and wanted to chat, along with fellow sailors from all over the place, but we decided that the nicest people of all were the harbour masters. They were invariably charming, incredibly helpful and were always willing to go out of their way to look after us. We were very grateful to them.

We were going to be staying in the Orkneys for three days and planned to widen our sphere a little by catching a bus to Kirkwall. From the bus, we were able to view the countryside from high up and get a real feel for the place. The highlight of Day 1 in the Orkneys had to be a visit to the Orkney Wireless Museum, which was surprisingly interesting. We also squeezed in a quick look round the History of the Orkneys Museum, the cathedral and found a jolly good café for lunch. The Orkneys were significant in that they were our pinnacle and our turning point. After the Orkneys, we would be turning south for the first time and heading for home. We needed to savour the experience.

Another Day Off

Arts and crafts proved to be quite a big thing in the Orkneys. The unadulterated beauty of the natural environment would inspire even an economist to reach for a paintbrush. I pointed this out to Bob (being both an economist and a philosopher), who said that so many of them painted and took up other creative pastimes because there was not a great deal else for people to do in these parts. Fair point, I thought. Philistine!

The artists and craftspeople of the Orkneys were very prolific, and some were obviously very successful, exporting what they make all over the world. Knitwear seemed to be a particularly big thing, as was silver jewellery. So many designs were based on all things connected to the sea. There were endless watercolours featuring sea views, and pottery made with images of fish. It all made complete sense, given that it was almost impossible not to see the sea without closing your eyes. It would have been very odd if they'd concentrated on the urban landscape.

The land in the Orkneys is apparently very fertile, but trees struggle to grow because of the fierce winds. We came across the occasional oak tree tucked into a dip or in a private sheltered garden, but otherwise it was bare. Tourism is a major part of the economy, but not in a pushy way. Visitors come to see wildlife, the many Neolithic sites and the Scapa Flow, which has its own dedicated visitor centre. The Neolithic village of Skara Brae has probably been one of the most exciting archaeological finds in Britain in the last century. It's an amazingly well-preserved settlement of houses and stone furniture that were found by chance in the 1920s, when a storm exposed them. There are also numerous sites of standing stones, the most well known being the Standing Stones of Stenness, which is a smaller version of Stonehenge and not crowded out by Druids. When we first arrived in the Orkneys, we thought that there wouldn't be much to see, but we loved it. We would have happily stayed for longer, but time and tide wait for no man and – as we were yet to discover – neither does the Pentland Firth.

Stromness to Wick (Homeward Bound)

Stromness was the pinnacle of our adventure by virtue of it being the furthest point north we would be venturing and, even more significantly, our turning point to go south towards home. Having made it so far in one piece, and having already stretched our horizons more than we ever imagined we could, we weren't remotely tempted to push our luck any further by carrying on to the remote Shetland Isles, which were ninety exposed nautical miles further north. Home was beginning to beckon gently, and we were ready to begin our journey down the long and rugged east coast of Great Britain.

When we first planned to head to the Orkneys, I'd assumed that leaving would involve just sailing on through the middle of the Islands and out the other side, thereby avoiding going through the notorious Pentland Firth. As previously mentioned, the Pentland Firth is the stretch of water between the Orkneys and the Scottish mainland, and at times it can be highly dangerous, particularly for small craft. This is all due to strong tidal currents and the uneven nature of the seabed, which can at times create unmanageably volatile seas.

Running north to south across the central part of the Pentland Firth (and not to be confused with a jolly band of travelling minstrels) is an area of exceptional turbulence called the Merry Men of Mey. Sometimes, these fellas Mey can manifest as a standing wave reaching up to thirty feet at its peak of horribleness. When it's in full flow, few ships of any size can pass without risking their safety. This is yet another fine example of giving a misleadingly cheery name to an inhospitable geographical feature; the Cape of Good Hope being another example. What a good thing we didn't have to go anywhere near it, I thought, rather naively.

When I finally pulled out our cargo-ship-sized chart to plan a safe and efficient passage, I could see what I thought looked like bridges linking the islands on the eastern edge of the Scapa Flow. I thought it was a bit odd that they hadn't put heights above sea level on the bridges, but assumed that they were bound to be high enough for most boats. Otherwise, how would anyone ever leave safely to go east?

After much scrutiny and investigation, the 'bridges' turned out to be thick and impenetrable low walls built by Churchill during the Second World War to keep German torpedoes out. They were known as the Churchill Barriers and were quite well known, it seemed. My heart sank.

We had two choices now, neither of which was in the original plan. One was to stay in the Orkneys forever, and the other was to face the watery equivalent of running the gauntlet by going through the dreaded Pentland Firth.

After some more slightly panicky research, I discovered that it was actually possible to travel through the Pentland Firth on a yacht and live, but only in the right conditions. The right conditions were a neap tide, wind of less than a Force 4, no swell to speak of and being present at a certain point just to the east of the Merry Men of Mey in time to catch the beginning of the east-going tide. We would be lucky to have all those favourable conditions coincide, but neaps was only three days away and the weather conditions were, for the moment, looking spot on. If weather conditions changed for the worse and it became too risky to leave on this occasion, we might have had to wait for another two weeks before the next neap tide but still wouldn't be able to guarantee getting calm enough weather.

Three days later, we hit the jackpot. The winds were gentle, visibility was acceptable and it was spot on neaps. We finally left the security of Stromness marina in a state of steadily increasing nervous tension and slowly made our way down through the channels between the islands of Hoy, Cava, Fara and Flotta, eventually turning west towards the recommended starting point just east of the Merry Men. The passage included catching a back eddy, which is a phenomenon caused as a tide going in one direction hits a bit of coastline and goes in the other direction from the main tidal stream.

As we sailed into the Pentland Firth, we made the gentle turn to the west, and as our speed over the ground increased we knew we had picked up the back eddy. Relief! That part of the passage plan was right! We looked out towards the Merry Men and they were lying quiet. Another relief. At the waypoint I'd put on the chart the night before, we made our turn east, hoisted the sails and, gradually carried by the full force of the east-going tide, *Bella Rosa* sailed serenely and safely out of the Firth between the islands of Swona and Stroma and towards the open sea. It was strange that we both now thought of the 'open' sea as safety! We passed Duncansby Head on the Scottish mainland to our west and, after another thirteen miles, we reached the north-east Scottish port of Wick. We were finally heading south and were homeward bound.

Although feeling jubilant, we were cold, tired and hungry when we arrived in Wick. There was also an unspoken touch of melancholy in the air that, even with several weeks to go and, no doubt, many adventures still to come, we were heading homewards and towards the end of this adventure. We were hugely grateful when several marina staff came out to assist us with the mooring. They were super friendly, very helpful and were obviously very proud of the service they provide. They even found someone to give Bob a lift to the local supermarket. It would be worth buying a boat and sailing into Wick marina purely to experience one of the warmest welcomes on the planet. We told them how nice we thought they were and they went off beaming.

Wick was a former herring fishery. They used to have an annual fishing festival and parade, and a herring queen would be crowned. They'd stopped the festival when the herring fishing industry ended but had recently reinstated the tradition. The newly appointed herring queen now gets brought into the harbour on the lifeboat. The annual event was due to take place during the following weekend but we would have moved on by then. We felt quite gutted that we were going to miss it!

The town itself had the look of a Lancashire mill town with its austere, factory-style buildings and tall, thin chimneys. Oddly, and rather enigmatically, it also had a bit of a continental feel about it, and not just because of the tricolour bunting they'd put up ready for their herring festival. Wick is apparently not a holiday destination; it's a functional working town and you can't buy a model puffin or novelty key ring anywhere. There were some postcards in one shop, but they were of Scrabster, which is at least thirty miles away. We must have been the nearest thing to a tourist that they'd ever had.

Wick to Peterhead

We spent one short night in Wick and hit the road again early the following morning. While heading out from Wick across the Moray Firth to Peterhead, I saw on the AIS what looked like a nameless cargo ship declaring itself to be doing 25 knots directly towards us. I could see the shape in the distance, and watched with both interest and even more than my usual high level of apprehension. Although it did seem to be getting closer, I was surprised that it wasn't transmitting its destination, size or purpose in life. It was quite some time before I realised that the cargo ship was actually a large oil platform, and we were getting closer to it rather than the other way round. I couldn't think why it would be transmitting a speed of 25 knots when it was firmly fixed to the seabed, but strange things happen at sea.

The passage to Peterhead started quite well because the sun was shining but, being a twelve-hour journey and having to be on deck much of the time, we became quite cold. By the time we reached Peterhead, we were feeling very weary and were wishing for better and warmer weather again. Jo, David and Graham had arrived in Peterhead from Whitehills earlier that day and had spotted us coming in on the AIS. They came over to help us moor up and to invite us over to *Dawn Treader* for a gin and tonic… or two. That was my idea of a support group.

Time Off in Peterhead

The top corner of north-east Scotland was cold, damp and windy, and it felt like it was midwinter. We were relieved not to be out on the water. I was feeling frozen to the core again and Bob had reverted to wearing long trousers. Despite the cold, the people of 'Peterrrhaird' smiled a lot. I think they were basking in what they classified as good summer weather. To alleviate the miseries of the biting wind, we went in search of our usual remedy: cake. In a place with a large and prominent prison complex and a multitude of austere-looking buildings, we didn't hold out much hope of finding a cake of a suitably high calibre. You can imagine our shock and delight when we came across the warm and inviting Mrs Bridges coffee shop. Their cakes were the best we'd come across since being in Ireland, and the orange and poppy seed slices quickly took our minds off the howling wind outside.

There was always something about each of our destinations that had made us think, or smile, or find inspiring. In the past, Peterhead had been home to four hundred fishing boats geared up to catching various sorts of white fish and herring. Nowadays, the fleet had been reduced to around seventy boats due to a combination of EU regulatory quotas and a sizeable reduction in fish stocks. The North Sea oil opportunity filled part of the employment gap and a lot of related activity was evident in the form of support boats and shore-based facilities. Despite the presence of all that, there was still a feeling that the once prosperous town was struggling economically.

The bad weather meant we would be spending a few days in Peterhead, so we needed to find some entertainment. The *Dawn Treader* crew brightly told us that they'd signed up for the guided tour of the prison, which loomed menacingly on the top of the cliff overlooking the marina. I was about to ask where we should buy the tickets when they all fell about laughing. How gullible can you get? Jollity aside, Peterhead prison has an ignominious reputation and has been dubbed 'the hate factory'. It is the home of some of the most reviled and dangerous sex offenders that have ever lived. The crimes committed by the inmates are so horrendous that, if hanging still existed, the prison would be empty. There had been a few escapes over the years and there was even a riot as recently as 1987, when a whole building was taken over and a prison officer was held hostage for five days until the SAS stormed in to take control. Would we be able to sleep peacefully in our beds that night?

There was plenty of evidence in Peterhead of the irrepressible human spirit. On the high street, we dropped into the Peterhead Project office, which also doubled as the tourist office, to ask what there was to do in the area. Along with being given some good ideas about how to spend our time, we were told in depth about their extensive work as a social enterprise. There were all manner of initiatives in place to keep the local population busy and involved with each other, and a strong support system available for small enterprises. The office was also a shop selling local produce, so we added our support by buying a jar of locally-made pickle.

The shops on the high street told their own stories about the nature of the inhabitants of Peterhead. There was the Peterhead Bait and Tackle and Knit Hoose (not a spelling mistake), an Eastern European minimarket called Oksana and an abundance of chiropodists. We noticed that the people of Peterhead were generally quite slim, and walked around very quickly with purposeful steps, often slightly hunched and leaning forwards as if to combat a cold, east wind blowing straight in from Siberia.

As far as finding things to do was concerned, they recommended that we should visit Slain's Castle near Crudeness Bay, and then walk to the nearby Kilmarnock Arms for a wee dram. The castle is reputed to have inspired Bram Stoker to write *Dracula*, and the pub was where he stayed when he wrote it. We were definitely up for that, even though it involved another bus ride.

Still in Peterhead

The next day, we caught the number 263 to Crudeness Bay to see Slain's Castle. We were going to follow in Bram Stoker's footsteps, but in reverse, as in visiting the pub first for a good lunch followed by a visit to the castle.

After lunch, we walked the mile to the castle along a rough track and came across it sitting in open land near the edge of a cliff. How refreshing it was to find that not only was there no visitor centre or charge to enter the castle grounds but there were also no concessions to health and safety either. There were no barriers, no danger notices, no legal warnings or yellow and black tape. There were wobbly stone walls, dodgy-looking arches, teetering turrets, precarious pathways and deep and treacherous precipices. Part of the castle was virtually hanging over the edge of the cliff. It was a lawsuit waiting to happen. How brilliant! It was like being a child again in the 50s and 60s, or being in Belgium.

There was no one else around and the castle was gratifyingly spooky. It was so creepy that I made sure I kept Bob within my sight the whole time. We were surprised that its tourist potential hadn't been even a tiny bit exploited because it surely would be a winner. Having said that, it was so enjoyable to be able to walk around something so old, dramatic and historically interesting completely unhindered. We'd eventually get over the disappointment of not being able to buy a Dracula tea towel or crucifix fridge magnet.

Even Longer in Peterhead

Plan A was to leave Peterhead on the Sunday morning but that would have entailed leaving at 3.00 a.m. to get to Arbroath by midday when the marina lock was open. Plan B was to stay in bed on the Sunday morning and go on the Monday instead. We opted for Plan B but still had to get going by 4.00 a.m. to get to Arbroath in time. Such is the life of the sailor.

A third day of rest was ahead of us and we were feeling much better for it. The highlight of our third day off was the short walk to the Spar minimarket attached to a nearby local garage; we felt that one visit to Peterhead town centre was quite sufficient in a lifetime. Once we'd located the entrance to the Spar, which was situated between a pizza take-out shed and a greasy spoon café, we managed to purchase a cucumber and some kitchen roll. This enabled us to create a Greek-style salad, but without the feta cheese, and wipe up efficiently afterwards (we already had some tomatoes). It can't all be high jinx and frivolity when you're living the nautical life.

The rest of the day was spent reading, relaxing and mulling over which ports we would stop at when we headed south from Peterhead. We were so looking forward to seeing Arbroath and trying out their famous smokies. After Arbroath would be Eyemouth and, after that, we'd be back in England for the first time in weeks and would have completely managed to escape being plagued by Scottish midges. They only had two more days to launch an attack before we crossed the border to safety.

Peterhead to Arbroath

No wonder they changed the name British Summer Time to Daylight Saving Time. Whoever came up with that outrageously misleading moniker was in danger of being sued for misrepresentation. We left Peterhead harbour at 4.30 a.m. in a hue of Daylight Saving Time grey, which, I thought, would have made a good Farrow and Ball paint colour name. As we motored along the coast, Slain's Castle was just about visible through the grey drizzle, and looked even spookier from the sea. It was enough to make the blood curdle. We agreed on doing hourly shifts in the cockpit so that whoever was off duty could get warm and dry down below.

I was wearing two pairs of socks, five tops, two pairs of thermal leggings, and had topped it all off with my full offshore set of foulies. There was no room inside the foulies for any more layers. Bob was even colder than me, which was unusual. He counted six tops, had put his waterproof salopettes over his trousers, and had his florescent yellow hood up. He talked about bacon sandwiches a lot until I eventually broke and went below to make the fantasy a reality. There is **nothing** like a hot bacon butty to lift the spirits when involved in jolly outdoor pursuits. They somehow never taste quite as good when eaten inside.

I'd left Bob on deck with his life jacket on and a Fastfind personal beacon tucked into his pocket. Never being one to be particularly afraid of death, he was prone to wandering about on deck without wearing any safety gear when I wasn't looking, so I decided to put a stop to it once and for all so that I could go below without worrying about whether he'd still be there when I went back up.

One of my worst sailing moments had actually come a year before our round Britain adventure when we were on passage to the Scilly Isles. I was down below in the saloon, 'off watch' and having a sleep, and Bob was in the cockpit on his own. As I said, Bob had a habit of moving about the deck doing this and that, which had always made me nervous. I had been asleep for an hour or so when a noise woke me up. I sat up and decided I'd go up and take a look. I emerged at the top of the companionway. No sign of Bob. I went the rest of the way into the cockpit to look around. Again, no sign of Bob. I looked behind the boat to see if I could spot a Bob overboard but it was difficult with the two metre swell. I called Bob's name at the top of my voice. We'd been motorsailing and the engine was doing about 2,200 revs, so it was quite noisy. I slammed the engine into neutral and then reverse and called again. I heard a muffled shout of "What the heck's going on?" from below. I looked into the saloon to see Bob, still on the 'throne', popping his head around the heads' door! I've never been so relieved in all my life. The noise I'd heard was Bob feeling the urgent call of nature, visiting the heads and accidentally letting the toilet seat drop rather noisily. He'd left *Bella Rosa* on automatic pilot and, given that we were in open water and the visibility was excellent, he didn't feel the need to disturb me for a three-minute break. But, that was the origin of our Fastfind rule!

Our destination was now Arbroath, the home of the famous Arbroath Smokie. There had been a TV programme about Arbroath, featuring a local man and smokery owner called Iain Spinks, who demonstrated how they were cooked. I couldn't wait to get to Arbroath to taste an authentic smokie.

The sun finally came out, and Arbroath appeared out

of the gloom like a chirpy little, brightly coloured toy town. It couldn't have been more different than Peterhead. Like many of the smaller harbours down the east coast of Britain, Arbroath is only accessible at certain times and in good weather conditions. The harbour is regulated by lock gates that only open for a short time either side of high water and, if there is even a small tidal swell, it wouldn't be safe to enter at all because the entry channel is narrow, exposed and lined with rocks. Naturally, we had done our usual forward planning and weather checking before setting off, but there is always an element of doubt when dealing with the elements and timing issues. The conditions turned out to be perfect. It was another of our lucky days!

Some harbours around Britain have live webcams trained on their entrances, probably so that people can check out the live sea state before venturing in or out. However, our friend Chris from Bath was using the service to do a bit of friendly spying on our movements, and he'd lined himself up to catch a 'screen grab' of us coming into Arbroath. We were instructed to wave as we came into the harbour, so we got a bit spruced up, brushed our hair and practised smiling in order to be camera ready. In the end, Chris managed to get four bird's-eye photos of us following the leading lines into the harbour and arriving. *Bella Rosa* looked great, but we needn't have worried how we looked because we weren't even visible.

The air in Arbroath was pungent with smells of smoked fish, and you could see the smoke curling its way out of the open windows of the small converted sheds at the bottom of the tiny, terraced, harbourside gardens. The practice of smoking haddock has been carried out in Arbroath since the 1820s, and each family has its own secret smoking methods. Pairs of haddock are tied together by their tails and suspended over square barrels containing a mixture of varieties of burning wood, and then cooked from between forty to sixty minutes. A recent EU directive states that Arbroath Smokies cannot be called Arbroath Smokies unless they have been smoked within five miles of Arbroath town centre. That seems reasonable enough.

We were advised that the best time to eat a smokie is straight from the oven, so we positioned ourselves in the nearby Spinks' family smokery in readiness to grab a large pair to take back to *Bella Rosa* for a lunchtime feast. We ate them in the traditional manner with our fingers, and were speechless with pure joy at how delicious they were. Our stomachs must have experienced a long delay in registering that they were adequately full because we mistakenly went back to purchase a second pair. Not surprisingly, we ended up feeling a bit nauseous, having worked our way through two large smoked haddocks each. Despite the gluttony, it had been worth the effort of travelling 1,600 nautical miles round Britain to get the chance to taste a fresh Arbroath Smokie on its own home ground. We were hooked, and even briefly considered moving to Arbroath to ensure a ready supply.

The rest of the day was dedicated to a walk around the town and surrounding countryside. Towards the end of the walk, we came across what must be one of the largest polytunnels we'd ever seen. It turned out to be East Seaton Farm, which had been created as a soft fruit farm in 1991 by Lochart and Debbie Porter. The exposed east coast of Scotland is the most obvious place to be producing late-season soft fruit and the Porters apparently spent some time trying different techniques to lengthen the natural growing season. They weren't able to find polytunnels on the market that would meet their needs so they developed their own 'Seaton system'. This was a low, pitched tunnel with the plastic actually ploughed into the soil to give extra strength and better sealing to maximise heat retention. This system allowed them to produce strawberries from early May and a second crop in late August, and raspberries from late May right through to the end of September. Great British ingenuity we thought! The workers were busy, diligently going about their tasks. As we left the farm and passed some bunkhouses, we noticed several cars with Eastern European number plates. The economics of Seaton Farm clearly didn't allow the Great Britishness to include the farm workers.

Arbroath to Eyemouth

Having cleared Arbroath out of smokies and found some East Seaton Farm strawberries, it was time to move on. Next stop was Eyemouth, which sounded like it would be full of eastern Scottish promise. It was yet another early morning start to be able to leave Arbroath before the lock gates shut and to get into Eyemouth before low tide, when it would be too shallow to enter the harbour.

Getting the timing right to leave one port in time to get to the next can be tricky, and the slightest swell from the wrong direction can prevent boats from entering or leaving many of the harbours along the east coast. It pays to plan where you wouldn't mind being stuck, so, once we'd seen Eyemouth, we knew it would be advisable to leave on the next suitable tide the following morning,

Eyemouth is a traditional and busy fishing port but appeared to be very run down. Even the large seaman's mission was empty and up for sale. The pilot book had stated that "the quayside taverns still reverberate with nautical swagger, so an amusing evening is guaranteed". We went in search of some of the nautical swagger and found that many of the taverns had gone out of business or were in desperate need of repair. We were quite relieved really, because it meant that we could go to bed early, but were a bit disappointed that our evening turned out to be less nautically amusing than we'd been led to expect.

Eyemouth to Amble

We were woken up very early by frenetic squawking. All the trawlers that we'd seen leaving the previous evening were returning and were being followed by hordes of hungry seabirds. The sun was out and the harbour had come alive as the trawlers tied up and offloaded their catch. The cheeky seagulls were swirling around madly or standing in droves on the quay walls, looking for a chance to grab an easy breakfast.

We needed to get out by 7.00 a.m. at the latest to have enough tide to allow us to sail over the sandbar at the entrance of the harbour. The presence of the sandbar explained the timing of the grand exodus of trawlers the previous evening and their return early that morning; they had the same tidal constraints as we did. Once out in the bay, the sea was lovely and calm. We had coffee on deck while we floated peacefully along the coast towards Amble. Sitting up in the cockpit first thing in the morning in the middle of a calm sea with no one else around is one of the many joys of life on the water. The seals were out in force and we couldn't help thinking that they have an enviable life of swimming or languishing lazily in the water and indulging in an endless supply of fish suppers.

We had a leisurely day ahead of us and hoped to anchor near the romantic-sounding Farne Islands for lunch. Instead of being the remote and spiritual idylls of our imagination, the Farne Islands were a swirling mass of squawking gannets and other seabirds. The smell of guano (seabird excrement, for the uninitiated) was so disgusting that we couldn't tolerate breathing the air around the islands for long, let alone eating our lunch there. We decided to carry on to Amble, and ate lunch on the move. We'd started out with just the motor on but the wind increased enough for us to sail smoothly along at a relaxing pace. From our 'gin and tonic' seats at the back of the boat, we were able to watch the soft, green and pleasant Northumbrian coastline go by with its numerous castles and endless sandy beaches. We finally crossed the invisible border back into English waters. The circle round the British Isles was being inexorably closed.

Amble was a surprising place. The Geordie accent was very strong and yet we were only forty miles from Scotland. The marina was friendly and attractive but in the town there were some tough-looking characters about, a few smashed windows, and many of the shops had metal shutters. Vandalism seemed to be a problem.

Amble used to be a coal mining town but the last colliery closed in the 1960s. After that, fishing returned as an important part of the economy. Looking at the number of expensive boats in the marina, there was obviously a contingent of wealthy people living in the area. The Amble Boat Company clearly catered to their needs as well as customers from further afield. Bob has a gillie friend, Iain, on the Tweed, where he goes salmon fishing. Iain is also a sailor with a lovely boat, *Aros More*, which was heartbreakingly torn from her swing mooring during a winter storm and smashed on to rocks. About the only boatyard that was able to carry out the repair was the Amble Boat Company. Happily, *Aros More* is now as good new.

We wanted to find out more about Amble's culture and history so planned a day off the following day to go on a big walkabout. First impressions can sometimes be deceptive.

Amble

It was pouring with rain so we ditched the idea of a long and bracing walk and decided to have a day of domesticity instead. Our domestic space, otherwise known as *Bella Rosa*, was a mere thirty feet by eight, so it was possible to move from one chore to another with just an extended stretch. Bob was wedged into our tiny galley, cooking a batch of three dinners Remoska style, and I went off to mess around with the marina washing machine. I also discovered that there was a proper bath in the ladies shower area and thus I was able to have my first bath since Dartmouth. I felt like a new woman after that!

I never really knew what constituted a Geordie, except that Cheryl Cole was one and Newcastle was somehow involved. It seemed like something we needed to know about so we looked it up. There are various theories about the origin of the term. One is that it referred to the supporters of King George II during the Jacobite revolution of 1745 and that it included those from Newcastle and the surrounding counties. Another theory is that when George Stephenson invented the miner's lamp in 1815 the miners from Newcastle who used them were subsequently called Geordies. These days, parochialists say that it's only those who live on the northern banks of the Tyne and within a mile of the city centre that are true Geordies. As far as we were concerned, it was all 'taramooosalorhta' to us and 'long live Ant and Dec', Lindisfarne, Gazza, half the cast of *Auf Wiedersehen Pet*, wearing Newcastle United shorts in Arctic conditions, and Newcastle Brown. I think I mentioned Cheryl Cole earlier.

After eating one of Bob's three Remoska dinners, we were feeling the need to stretch our legs. It was a bit foggy outside but the rain had reduced to a drizzle. We walked along the riverbank to Warkworth Castle in the ancient town of Warkworth. Warkworth is a small town, bursting with ancient character with its thriving olde worlde pubs and well-appointed bed and breakfasts. We went for a drink in one of the pubs to dry off, and managed a few games of pool before heading back home along the riverbank. Warkworth proved to be definitely worth the walk.

Amble to Tynemouth (Newcastle)

The plan was to get up early to check out the conditions before committing ourselves to leaving Amble. There was no sign of the crew of *Dawn Treader*, who had arrived the previous evening. We'd noticed that they had a tendency to appear on deck about two minutes before leaving, still clutching a mug of tea and looking like they weren't about to go anywhere, then, before you had time to ask "What time are you off?" they'd cast off and were gone. How laid back can you get?

Our verdict was that, as it wasn't too windy, and as the fog had lifted, it was all stations go to Newcastle. The sea on the route out through the Amble estuary was flat and calm but, as we approached the two pier heads at the entrance to the harbour, it transformed into a quite substantial swell. It was just after high tide, so there was no danger of us hitting the bottom in one of the troughs of each wave, but an hour later it would have been too dangerous to attempt to leave.

It was only twenty nautical miles to the Tyne so it was going to be an easy day for us. We had a quiet few hours sailing but knew we were approaching the industrial north when we were followed up into Newcastle harbour by a huge cargo ship. Once inside the harbour, we were told off very politely by the port authorities for not asking permission to enter. We must have missed the small print in the almanac. We could see the point of it. It could be very risky for a small boat to get in the way of something so huge with limited manoeuvrability. Size does matter. We stuck a Post-it note up on the wall to remind ourselves to ask permission to leave when the time came.

The Tyne was such an easy harbour to enter after all the complicated pilot plans we'd needed so far down the east coast. The main channel is wide and accessible at all states of the tide, and so is the marina. The Royal Quays marina at North Shields had a lock at the entrance but they open it as and when people need it, twenty-four hours a day. Being on the north side of the Tyne, we were in proper Geordie territory. We wanted to spend a few days in the area and, given that we were only two or three weeks away from the finish, were going to start easing ourselves back into normal life. We would start the following morning in Newcastle city centre with a trip to the cinema and a mooch around Marks & Spencer. Long live North Shields, polite officials with Geordie accents on Channel 16, Gazza, Cheryl Cole...

A Day Out In Newcastle

Bob had a conference call to make so I left him behind on *Bella Rosa* while I went in search of some retail therapy in the centre of Newcastle. It was a strange feeling branching out by myself after us being virtually fused together for the last ten weeks. The way to get to the centre of town was via the metro, and the nearest station was a twenty-minute walk from the marina. I crossed over the marina lock and carried on through some well-designed and attractive housing developments joined up by a web of pathways and thoughtful landscaping.

Before long, I found myself in the middle of a fairly secluded park, and suddenly felt very vulnerable. Remembering that after ten weeks of living on a boat I probably resembled a deranged bag lady, I assumed that no one would be remotely interested in coming anywhere near me, let alone run off with my small, but deceptively capacious, backpack. In the state I was in, I was more likely to have money pressed into my hand by a worthy community-conscious soul than to be mugged. Even so, I hid my phone and purse in an inside jacket pocket. I was, after all, in unfamiliar territory, and the general mood of things was hard to gauge.

I plucked up courage to ask a man accompanied by four boisterous dogs of varying denominations the way to the nearest metro station. He told me the direction and laughed, saying "Don't forget to watch out for the Apaches". I had no idea what he was talking about, but smiled knowingly and said that I would indeed watch out for them. Sitting on Meadow Well station platform, I kept a close watch for anyone resembling a Native American but got the whole way to the centre of Newcastle without encountering even one.

It was only when Googling 'Newcastle' later that evening that I discovered that Meadow Well is as rough an area as you can get. It was the site of the infamous Meadow Well riots in 1991 that followed the deaths of two local youths killed in a car crash involving a police chase. There are gangs, and people get robbed. I guessed at that point that the Apaches was probably the name of a local gang. All that well-tended foliage made the true nature of the area quite deceptive. When Bob joined me later in the city, he said he'd felt quite threatened while standing on the station platform despite the fact they'd tried to make it look cheerful and safe by painting it in sunshine yellow. On another occasion, perhaps wearing Newcastle United shorts would be a good idea.

Emerging from the metro at the Monument was like returning to earth after a long voyage in intergalactic space. I just stood there and slowly took in my surroundings with awe and wonder. There were all the familiar shops that are to be found on every high street in England, but the setting was strikingly grand. Newcastle turned out to be a handsome city with a prevalent Georgian influence. It was simply magnificent!

A good mooch was in order, followed by a culture fix at the Laing Art Gallery. When Bob arrived several hours later, we decided to go to the Gate multi-screen cinema complex to see a film. We each had a preference for a different film so solved any potential disagreement by watching two consecutively. After all, we'd been starved of that kind of entertainment for such a long time. The Gate had everything a self-respecting Geordie would want for a great night out. Along with umpteen cinemas, there was the

Orbit night club, Nando's, Pizza Hut and McDonalds. There were stag parties, hen parties and groups of pub crawlers in various states of dress, undress and raucousness. Newcastle on a Saturday night! You can't beat it!

Trouble was obviously expected to brew fairly early in the evening, judging by the number of police cars and ambulances hovering in readiness by only 6.00 p.m. (In Bath, the police don't usually arrive until 11.00 p.m.). Unlike other European nationalities, I have never felt that British girls have much idea about how to look glamorous and sexy, and the girls of Newcastle were no exception. The prevalent look was having as much flabby flesh as possible hanging over and out of blood-circulation-stopping bits of thin material. The resulting edifice was propped up by towering stiletto heels sharp enough to be classified as a weapon. None of them could walk properly, so, when the fire alarm went off in the complex, no one was capable of responding because they clearly weren't prepared to ditch the shoes. It was a good job it was a false alarm.

We thought it was best to give the hordes of revellers a wide berth for various reasons, not least the fear of being stabbed in the foot by one of those stilettos. The men, by contrast, looked pretty ordinary – but hardy – in their sleeveless T-shirts and jeans or baggy shorts. They were huddled together in little support groups as if they were also in fear of being fatally stabbed in the foot or maybe even the neck if things turned a bit sour later in the evening. The predatory female, it seems, is alive and well and living in Newcastle. We couldn't resist taking some photos but tried to do it from a secluded doorway so we wouldn't incur anyone's wrath. We left the centre of Saturday-night Newcastle unscathed and returned to *Bella Rosa* to plan our exodus the following morning to the well-known seaside resort of Whitby. The best fish and chip shop in Britain was beckoning.

Tynemouth To Whitby

We arrived in Whitby in time to check out whether Rick Stein was right about the Magpie Café being the best fish and chip restaurant in the UK. As we'd done a fair bit of research into fish and chip dinners since setting off back in April, we felt that we could say with authority that it was a justified accolade. It wasn't just a case of cod, haddock or plaice with your chips; there was monkfish, halibut, Dover sole, sea bass, brill, gurnard, hake, mackerel, scampi, salmon, John Dory, plaice, lemon sole, skate wing and something called 'woof'. Woof is apparently sea cat and tastes like a cross between haddock and cod (and not a slice of man's best friend thrown in to mollify the meat eaters). There was even a choice of batter; gluten free being one of the choices. It took quite a while just to read the menu but, after being tempted to try the woof and chips, I chickened out and settled for my old favourite: sea bass.

We would have liked to spend a few days in Whitby, but I had a nagging feeling that we should leave the following evening at the latest to sail through the night to Lowestoft. When I woke up the following morning, the feeling was still there, so I poured over the weather forecasts and tide tables to get as much hard evidence as possible to back up those feelings. Stronger winds, mist and fog were predicted within a day or so, and we didn't want to risk a night sail along an inhospitable and busy coastline in poor visibility and gusty winds. Tougher conditions would also mean that both of us would need to be on duty together throughout the night for safety's sake. That was a very exhausting prospect. The least journey time to Lowestoft was going to be twenty-four hours, and we wanted it to be as trouble free as possible with the opportunity to get a few hours' sleep. Access to Whitby harbour was dependent on tidal heights, so we weren't going to be able to leave Whitby until the bridge opened at seven o'clock that evening. We prepared as much as we could for the journey and then went off to enjoy the rest of the day in Whitby.

Having never been to Whitby before, it was fun to be able to spend the day being tourists in an ancient town full of old cobbled streets and steeped in history. The main part of the town is wrapped around a large bustling harbour of historic maritime significance. Shipbuilding, herring fishing and whaling had been an important part of the economy, and it was in Whitby in the 1700s that Captain Cook first felt the lure of the sea as a merchant navy apprentice. The Captain Cook Tour, taken on a replica miniature galleon – but presumably without the weevils, rats, and scurvy – was a popular attraction. Being in a seafaring state of mind, we spent some of our time in a great little RNLI museum paying homage to the latter-day lifeboatmen of the wild Yorkshire coast. It was full of old and grainy photos showing the rugged faces of the brave local men, who'd volunteered to risk their lives in flimsy wooden lifeboats and treacherous seas to help save others. It reminded us yet again of how extraordinary the human spirit can be, and how grateful we were to know that the RNLI were on call in case of emergency while we were out there on the ocean taking chances.

Whitby isn't all about the sea; it also has a strong literary and religious heritage, including being the home of Caedmon, the earliest known Anglo-Saxon poet. Elizabeth Gaskell's novel, *Sylvia's Lovers*, was set in Whitby, and Charles Dickens and Wilkie Collins stayed there and probably couldn't resist penning a few meaningful lines at the same time. Bram Stoker based some of *Dracula* in Whitby, probably in St Mary's churchyard at night.

We carried on in order to take a look at the impressive ruins of the thirteenth-century Whitby Abbey, which overlook the town from the East Cliff. The Abbey is sited alongside the ancient church of St Mary's at the top of what they call the '199 Steps'. I was happy to discover that I had no trouble walking up them, despite the fact that my muscle mass must have dwindled to nothing after ten weeks of being confined on a boat. Bob sprang up them like a gazelle and was waiting at the top for me, so nothing had changed in that respect either.

The Abbey, which must have been magnificent in its day, had been highly influential in forming the Christian church. It was at the Synod of Whitby in AD 664 that the discussion took place about how the different strands of Christianity could be brought together as one cohesive system, rather than be fragmented and in conflict with each other. Whitby Abbey has to be one of the most interesting ruins in the whole of Great Britain. We were reluctant to leave but vowed to come back one day by car and spend more time there.

Along with the profound religious heritage, Whitby offered something else which was completely unique. It was the centre of jet mining, a gemstone which is the product of the fossilised remains of a type of tree from the Jurassic period only to be found on a seven-and-a-half-mile stretch of the Yorkshire coastline centred around Whitby. Mining jet and making it into jewellery, ornaments and other artefacts has been part of Whitby's economy for hundreds of years, and it was particularly popular in Victorian times. Whitby jet is such an important part of Whitby's history that it has its own dedicated heritage centre, and the shops are full of it. After we left, I regretted not buying something made from jet as a memento, which is another very good reason why we will have to return one day.

An Overnight Sail From Whitby To Lowestoft

Sometimes with sailing it can be a case of once you've set off you are committed to the passage and there can be no going back. Whitby was a good example of all or nothing. The swing bridge was only ever open two hours either side of high water and, after our departure, would soon be closed for eight hours. We had to very be sure we were making the right decision to go because our only viable refuge en route was the Humber River, which – we had on good authority – was a dangerous prospect with its constantly shifting sandbanks and fast-flowing tides. We'd been strongly advised to avoid it. There were no suitable places of refuge on the Norfolk coast either, so it looked like we were bound for Lowestoft, a twenty-four-hour access harbour on the coast of Suffolk.

In addition to it being a long and tricky passage, Whitby to Lowestoft was going to be the first night sail we'd ever done by ourselves. We needed to be on high alert! We motored out between the two imposing old pillars that marked the entrance of Whitby harbour and turned south. As day moved into night, we were blessed with a spectacular bright orange sunset that faded slowly down to a dark burnt sienna colour, before becoming deep mid blue and then the inevitable near jet black, dotted by a few tiny shore lights.

Our night hours were to be spent along a stretch of coastline we judged would be quite quiet. How wrong could we be! When I emerged, still feeling dozy, at one o'clock in the morning to start my night shift, we appeared to be surrounded by dozens of huge cargo ships. Bob, who had been on the case for three hours by then, reassured me that many of them were in fact at anchor and, as they were also lit up like Christmas trees, were easy to avoid.

There were, however, a few big ships making their way up and down the coast, and they needed to be watched very closely. In the three hours I was on watch, I had to change course twice to avoid ships that were heading directly for us. Luckily, my manoeuvres seemed to be effective because we managed to miss them by a decent margin. From time to time, a large ship would alter course to overtake us from behind but, again, they were never too close for comfort. In the end, it all made complete sense and there was nothing to worry about.

Despite enjoying my session of sailing in the dark, the glow of sunrise as we approached the Humber area was a welcome sight. It was almost as lovely as the sunset the night before but was accompanied by an added sense of relief at having survived the night in what turned out to be an unexpectedly busy waterway. In some ways, when sailing among other boats a night sail is more straightforward than a day sail. Everyone has to show specific lights so that you know what they are and where they are in relation to you. Big ships at anchor are required to switch on all their deck lights and you can see whether ships in transit are on collision course by the position of their lights. The great thing about a night sail in the summer is that the night doesn't last very long. It didn't go dark until 10.30 p.m., and by 3.00 a.m. there was a thin strip of light forming on the horizon in the east. Our night sail was actually quite enjoyable and the bacon rolls at dusk helped enormously in keeping up general morale.

The seas became less busy as we approached the Norfolk coastline, but a fine veil of mist had established itself, and visibility was reduced to a couple of miles at the most. Unexpectedly, the blades of a huge windmill appeared through the mist on our port side, followed by many more, as a wind farm, clearly in the early stages of construction, began to reveal itself. This hadn't been marked on our charts and could have posed a major problem if we'd come across it in the dark, even if it had been well lit. We might have thought we had a huge fleet of big cargo ships bearing down on us. We'd read that once a wind farm had been completed it was permissible to sail among the turbines because the blades are supposed to be a lot higher than the average boat mast. I resolved never to put it to the test, although I could imagine the challenge would appeal to Bob.

We skirted the coast of Norfolk, keeping fairly close to the shore. The wind had been steadily picking up from the south, so we were making a good 6 knots and arrived at Lowestoft by seven o'clock that evening, having had a manageable twenty-four-hour journey with no unexpected tricky moments. We were very tired, but it's easy enough to keep going without much sleep when you know it's only going to be for twenty-four hours. It wasn't a journey we would ever wish to repeat but mainly because we'd seen enough of the east coast by boat, and it's not an easy coast to sail. Any future visits would have to be by car. Having said that, it had been a valuable part of our challenge, and we felt that we'd learnt even more about the varieties of sea states and sailing conditions you can encounter, and the criteria for good decision making.

A Day Off to Recover
In Lowestoft

Lowestoft is a great place to stop, if you have to. We were at Britain's most easterly point, and had gone from Geordie to Yorkshire to Cockney in two large steps. There was something very familiar about being in Lowestoft despite the fact it was our first visit, and we had a strong impression of being near the end of our journey.

After successfully surviving the Whitby to Lowestoft passage, we felt that we'd nearly done all the really big sailing stuff (by our standards), but we still had to cross the Thames estuary. At the outset, crossing the Thames estuary sounded like it might be an ordeal, but by now we were fairly relaxed about the prospect. Once we reached the other side of the estuary, we would be in familiar waters, having sailed that way on *Bella Rosa* when we brought her back from Holland. A lot of water had passed under the keel since then. In fact, we calculated more than 2000 nautical miles.

Lowestoft marina is the sister marina to the Lowestoft Haven marina, which is several miles away down river. It's mainly just an annex that used to be called the Hamilton Dock and was used to accommodate only fishing fleets and commercial ships. Lowestoft had been another thriving fishing port that was now struggling. Whenever we wanted any help from the marina staff, we had to phone the main marina, and someone would eventually come over by launch. They had to make a special trip just to bring me a token for the washing machine, and then had to make another trip back again with a replacement token after I'd realised that I'd jammed the mechanism with the first token! When I suggested it might be easier for them if the machines ran on pound coins, they said that they couldn't risk it as it was rather a remote area and a hotbed of potential crime. We decided it was best not to dwell on that too much but couldn't help noticing that we were surrounded by corrugated iron roofs, warehouses, cranes, a wind turbine, several large, metal storage tanks and that there was no one else around apart from us and the token man.

Lowestoft's original old high street looked like it had seen better days, and a more modern street of shops had been established nearby. We didn't think the new street looked much better – despite the bunting – but we were enjoying being somewhere a bit different. The weather was quite warm, and we were also enjoying wearing T-shirts for the first time since being in the west of Scotland. It was great to have reached Lowestoft and have a rest, but we were keen to move on to Shotley, which was to be our next port of call.

Lowestoft to Shotley

Our friends, Janene and Jules, keep their boat, *Temptress*, in Shotley marina, and we'd spent a wonderful weekend on her with them a couple of years previously. They were both highly experienced sailors, and Janene had even been on one of those round-the-world races that takes nine months or so to complete. They were planning on coming on board *Bella Rosa* with us for a day or two to try her for size, and I was hoping they would agree to take over the running of things and allow me to relinquish responsibility for a while.

On our way to Shotley, despite predictions of quite gusty winds, we had a really great sail past the flat Suffolk coastline. There was little to see apart from a glimpse of the Sizewell nuclear power station that loomed out of the mist that shrouded the shoreline. It looked like something out of a science fiction film.

Safely entering the Felixstowe and Harwich area requires that you follow a designated route just outside the main shipping lanes. It's a very busy commercial shipping port, and it's wise to steer clear of the bigger traffic. We formed a crocodile with a few other yachts that were following the same route, and weaved our way up to Shotley to meet Janene and Jules. They were waiting to take our lines in the marina.

We spent the rest of the evening eating and drinking and talking non-stop boat talk, which wasn't difficult after living on one for nearly three months. We could see that we could end up being the biggest boat bores ever when we returned home.

Janene and Jules were all set to come with us on *Bella Rosa* the following day and were planning to take us around some of their favourite local haunts. I announced that I was demoting myself to general dogsbody while we were in their home waters. My brain was going to have a blissful day off at last while they made all the important decisions and told me what to do.

Hearing the shipping forecast always stirs the imagination and by the time we'd reached Lowestoft we'd sailed through about half of the UK sea areas. We'd started in Wight and had carried on through Portland, Plymouth, Fastnet, Lundy, Malin, Hebrides, Fair Isle, Cromarty, Forth, Tyne and Humber. Thames would be the last shipping area we would travel through before entering Wight again. When we heard the Thames coastguard for the first time over the radio in Shotley, we realised just how far we'd come and how close we were now to the end of our odyssey.

Shotley to Pinmill with Janene and Jules

Before setting sail, Janene and Jules took us up to a large and exotic food hall, which involved going in a car for the first time in weeks, and presented us with a rare bulk-buying opportunity. We started by having coffee and the inevitable cake in the attached garden centre, and then wandered among the tastefully laid-out counters burgeoning with some of the best local produce Suffolk could offer. Between us, we accumulated a wide range of naughty treats and delicious goodies to see us through the weekend. Once we'd offloaded the spoils, we braced ourselves for a brisk sail out of the estuary to see how the sea was behaving. It was very gusty and blowing up to an occasional Force 6, but I wasn't in charge and could allow myself to be pleasantly oblivious. Upwind, the going was quite hard work so we didn't stay out in the open sea for long. A more relaxing option was to find ourselves a buoy at Pin Mill and visit the Butt and Oyster pub for dinner.

We had a lovely sail up the wide and accommodating River Stour and, although it was still a bit gusty, the estuary offered more shelter than out in the open sea. We found our buoy, put the kettle on and worked our way steadily through cake, scones and jam, followed by gin and tonics, before taking the dinghy over to the pub. The Butt and Oyster not only had a charming and unusual name but also had a great reputation in the area for good, honest food and a traditional east-coast pub ambience. It certainly lived up to it. The setting was unspoilt, with far-reaching views across the river, which was lined with houseboats that people actually lived on. There was a strong sense of community among the houseboat owners, and it seemed like an uncomplicated and easy-going life to lead.

The nearby sailing club was going to be hosting the 51st annual Thames barge race on the Saturday morning, and all the participants were congregating in the river ready for the race the following morning. There are only thirty authentic Thames barges left in existence, and seventeen of them were going to be taking part in the race. We learnt that the barges originated in the 1800s and early 1900s as working cargo vessels. They were designed to be sailed by just a man and a boy, presumably so that father and son could work together and not be dependent on a crew. The flat hulls were designed to deal with the shallow waters of the Thames estuary, and could carry anything from linseed to manure.

On the way back from the Butt and Oyster, our outboard motor decided to conk out, so Janene and I insisted on rowing us all the way back to *Bella Rosa*. *Swallows and Amazons* is nothing compared to what we'd been up to.

From Pin Mill Back to Shotley

Being able to wake up moored in the middle of a delightful estuary on a warm and sunny morning is one of the best things about life on a boat. Our lazy day started with breakfast on deck in the sun, a walk along the riverbank and then a short sail back to Shotley marina. It was breezy, but the sun was out, and we revelled in the feeling of the wind in our hair as we glided under sail down the river.

In the evening, we all moved over to *Temptress*, where Janene and Jules produced a bottle of champagne to celebrate having made it so far, and Janene cooked us pasta with mozzarella and chorizo. We were almost delirious with happiness.

A Day Off In Suffolk

It was such a novelty being back on land with ready access to a car, and with people who knew what was what in the area. A large poster announced that there was a Bluegrass music festival happening nearby and, as there's nothing like indulging in a bit of indigenous culture when travelling, we decided it was not to be missed. By the time we'd finished our slow pootle around endless pretty Suffolk lanes, the festival had almost finished, but we still managed to catch a performance by Suffolk's answer to the Foggy Mountain Boys twanging their English cowboy hearts out.

After indulging in a bumper-sized, locally-made ice cream each, we carried on with our whistle-stop tour of other worthwhile areas of east Suffolk. This involved having to prise ourselves out of the increasingly comfortable car to walk for a prolonged period at a thirty-five degree angle around the slippy grassy perimeter of the large and impressive medieval Framlingham Castle. Even at the time the walking was quite hard work, but the impending lopsided stiffness that we knew would strike us the following morning made it very tempting to walk all the way back in the opposite direction to even things up a bit. That's sightseeing for you. Despite the prospective left leg ache, we agreed that having a good walk had been a great idea, and it was satisfying to be outside among some inland ancient heritage.

Janene and Jules had recommended that, before leaving the area, we should take *Bella Rosa* a little way back up north again and visit Orford, a quaint little town tucked a long way up the tortuously narrow River Ore estuary. Given that it was well known for its continuously shifting sandbanks and tight entrance, J and J were concerned that we may have trouble safely negotiating it without some expert input. They insisted on accompanying us to the shore above the entrance so that we could see exactly what we were letting ourselves in for. We were then issued with full instructions on how to avoid disaster. It certainly made a change from having to arrive somewhere new with only the information provided by a pilot book and a chart. We were looking forward to giving it a go and, after all the detailed advice, had no excuse if we ended up getting stuck.

Sadly, our time with Janene and Jules was coming to an end; they needed to get back to the real world of work. We were on our own once again. What a fantastic weekend it had been discovering the joys of the Suffolk countryside with two enthusiastic and fun friends and relearning the art of human communication. It had been excellent preparation for our imminent re-entry into normal society.

Shotley to Pin Mill Again
(Because it Was so Nice)

The rivers and creeks along the east coast of England are extensive, and local knowledge is advisable in order to negotiate them safely. The changing nature of the River Ore is a typical example. These rivers can wind their way inland for miles and are the essence of Suffolk. Travelling the estuaries by boat has so much to offer in the way of wildlife, villages, communities and fabulous scenery and, as a sailing experience, it differs widely from coast hopping from port to port. To me, the county of Suffolk seemed to be all about detail. The longer we spent there – and the more familiar it became – the better it appeared to get. Being in Suffolk was like being embedded is an enormous Constable painting full of perfect cottage gardens. It's English to the core, and largely unspoiled, with the prettiest of villages and heart-stopping countryside. There were fields and hedgerows of bright red poppies everywhere, and wild flowers of all sorts lined every country road. An added bonus for me was seeing my first live hare, which leapt across the road in front of us as we were driving along. Although the hare can represent many things in mythology, its appearance on a classic English summer day in the heart of Suffolk was an affirmation to me of all that typified Englishness. This was England at its very best.

    After our friends had left, we were reluctant to leave Shotley, Pin Mill and the River Stour. It was just so nice. We motored out of Shotley marina and went back up the river to Pin Mill to find a mooring buoy for the night and with the intention of revisiting the enticing Suffolk Food Hall the following day. Visiting the food hall was becoming an addiction but we felt that a third visit – including lunch – might finally get it out of our system. What a shame we had to resort to getting a bus, and were therefore limited by how much we could carry, but it's surprising how many bags of shopping can be transported by hand by two extremely determined people.

In the end, we came away with enough food for a three-day gourmet standard siege and collapsed in exhaustion back on *Bella Rosa*, unfit for anything other than spending the rest of the day lying on deck with a book in the warm breeze. Bob was to cook a gas-cooker-style evening meal and produced a delicious salad with lightly grilled halibut and sliced, herby chips. What better proof that he had become extraordinarily versatile in the cuisine department? I happily did the washing-up.

Pin Mill to Orford

We weren't the only ones slipping off mooring buoys at six-thirty the next morning; there were seven other yachts preparing to leave. We were hoping they weren't all heading towards Orford and speeded up as much as possible in case they were and there was limited space once we got there. It was a case of looking after number 1. However, we didn't need to worry because they scattered in all directions once we were out of the estuary, and we thankfully travelled north unaccompanied. It wasn't the first time we'd backtracked on this trip. The previous time was when we were heading south for the Caledonian Canal from the Outer Hebrides, did a three-point turn in the middle of the Sound of Mull and ended up going to Cape Wrath instead. No such momentous decisions were made this time. Orford was only fifteen miles north of Harwich and was only a little tricky to negotiate – as opposed to downright scary. After visiting Orford, we would be pointing *Bella Rosa* south again towards home.

Due to the shallow seabed, it's only possible to enter or leave the River Ore two hours either side of high water, so we had timed our journey accordingly. I'd noticed that Bob seemed particularly drawn to the idea of sailing up the Ore, but I suspected that it was more likely to be the lure of dodging treacherous sandbanks than viewing the surrounding grassland or unusual bird life. There'd been quite a build-up prior to this endeavour, so I was a little nervous about doing it, but keen to see what all the fuss was about.

In addition to the extensive verbal instructions about how to negotiate the entrance to the Ore, Janene and Jules had given us two A4 sides of printed notes stating the current position of the channel marker buoys and the best course to take between them. I felt that I was so well primed by now that I could take a high level qualification on the subject. We'd also been briefed not to allow ourselves to be freaked out by a vigorously swirly bit of water that usually manifests itself just beyond the main entrance. It was harmless and should be ignored, we were told. We set off on our mission, stuck firmly to the plan and in the end it was literally plain sailing. The remaining river was beautifully tranquil and a conveniently vacant visitor buoy was waiting for us quite close to the village quay.

We had to go by dinghy to get to the quay, as there wasn't a regular water taxi, but our outboard motor was now sounding like a sheep with a sore throat. It had conked out previously when we were in Pin Mill, and we were constantly suspicious of it but decided to carry on to the village quay regardless. We managed to get to the village and back without any mishaps but decided against a return trip for dinner later that evening just in case our luck ran out. Just to make matters worse, one of the rollocks on the dinghy had now sheared off so we couldn't even row properly. If the engine conked out, the least likely place we would end up would be back on *Bella Rosa*, and neither of us fancied spending a night on the nearby nature reserve despite the rich variety of birds and wildlife.

Orford is yet another fiercely quaint place made up of numerous quintessentially English cottages adorned with roses. It was a great time of year to visit because all the flowers were at their blooming best and framing every doorway. When it dawned on me that the cottages weren't actually thatched, I wondered if that made them any less quintessential, which would mean that they would have to be described as quintelessessential.

We strolled around the pretty streets and discovered a castle, three pubs, a general store and a smart delicatessen. The general store was also a post office and a café so we stopped for a cup of tea and sat outside until the smoke from someone's bonfire completely obscured the view. Either there were no rules in Orford about acceptable times to have bonfires or it was clear proof that a subversive element exists in every community, however small and seemingly righteous. Back in the safety and fresh air of our seaside home, *Bella Rosa*, we settled down for a quiet rest and reviewed what was in the fridge. Orford was but a brief encounter, but a pleasant one. We were in awe of the Ore.

From Orford Back to The River Stour

We'd successfully negotiated the entrance to the Orford River but also had to plan our exit carefully. We needed to leave Orford at 9.00 a.m. to have enough tide to cross the entrance without bashing the bottom. We had wanted to visit West Mersea, but the timing was all wrong to get over the shallow sandbar at that entrance. This was a typical scenario in this part of the world. Revisiting the River Stour was a good alternative, but we needed provisions and, once we'd left the Ore, we decided to go back to Harwich to tie up on the town pontoon in order to go in search of fresh bread.

The backstreets of Harwich are made up of wonky, old seafaring houses and historical pubs. It was so atmospheric that it was easy to imagine the days of old when press gangs were operating. Idiosyncratically, there were several Chinese restaurants housed in Tudor buildings, and antiquarian bookshops wedged between tattoo parlours. We couldn't find anywhere that sold bread but decided that it didn't matter because it was a lovely, breezy, English summer's day and delightful to be out and about on foot.

We went back on board, set sail and ambled slowly down the coast while basking in the sunshine, with our goal for the day being to moor on a buoy further down the river. The Stour and the Orwell are both wide, very easy to navigate and incredibly peaceful considering they are so close to the busy ports of Felixstowe and Harwich. Despite the fact that it was July and the weather was lovely, there were very few other yachts about. It was surprising that it was so easy to escape the crowds when being so close to London and the south coast, but we weren't complaining.

The River Stour to Ramsgate

Crossing the Thames estuary was always going to involve some serious forward planning. Harwich to North Foreland Point is a wide stretch of hazardously busy waterway of about thirty-four nautical miles as the crow flies. If we were able to sail shore to shore, the journey would take us around six hours, but the eastern part of the estuary is strewn with long sandbanks extending menacingly out towards the open sea, and assiduously careful navigation is essential. Having to negotiate the sandbanks would mean we would be kept out 'on the battlefield' for quite a long time and would be exhausted by the time we reached Ramsgate, which was our next port of refuge.

The navigable channels that lead the way through the Thames have fascinating names like 'Black Deep', 'Knock Deep', 'King's Channel' and 'Wallet'. The larger channels are dissected by smaller channels known as 'gats', which enable you to work your way across steadily but in a rather circuitous fashion. All the channels are well marked with buoys so, if the weather is acceptable and the tides are heading in the right direction, they shouldn't pose a problem, provided of course that you can see where you are going.

There are many different recommended routes across the Thames estuary, and we chose the one that takes you right round the eastern edge of the main sandbanks, skirting the most northerly tips of some of them. We slipped our mooring at 5.30 a.m. and sailed east to round a cardinal buoy called 'Cork Hole', after which we would turn south across the busy waterway before rounding the northern tip of Black Deep to catch the flood tide down towards Ramsgate.

I'd peppered the chart plotter and our paper charts with waypoints at all the significant buoys. I'd worked out a highly detailed passage plan and felt confident that our journey should be relatively straightforward. The forecast was for pleasant weather, after an early morning mist that would clear within an hour or two of setting off. After that, visibility was predicted to be good enough for crossing the main estuary. As we left our mooring, the light mist over the Stour already looked like it was burning off in the early morning sun and, as we left the harbour entrance – which we now knew by heart – the sun was still glimmering strongly behind the haze. We foresaw no problems.

By the time we reached Cork Hole, things weren't looking so great. The sun had completely disappeared and thick fog was beginning to set in. We were by now fully committed to carrying on because turning back would have involved sailing into a strong, adverse tide, and would mean we would make little headway. Our foghorn, radar and AIS were at the ready and we were both on full alert. There's something so unreal and tempered about sailing in fog that it's almost quite pleasant. Serenity was a misguided state of mind under the circumstances, but at least it prevented us from panicking.

We rolled away our headsail and switched on the motor to give us a clearer view of what was in front of us, and to be prepared for quick action if we needed it. Our foghorn was so loud that we were almost disorientated every time we sounded it. I'd managed to temporarily deafen the Admirable by doing my first practice blast right next to his ear. This didn't go down that well, but it had the advantageous effect of persuading him to get a move on with putting on his life jacket after I threatened to do it again unless he complied. I made a mental note to get one for use during domestic negotiations at home.

We started to hear the regular, low, deep moan of a foghorn on our port side. Once we'd got the hang of using our own foghorn, we sounded our own requisite one prolonged blast every two minutes. It was a relief to discover that the other sound was coming from a fixed fog beacon and wasn't actually another boat. We'd eventually been able to identify it by the sequence of blasts it was emitting, and it helped to confirm our position on the chart.

Things seemed to be going quite well despite the visibility being down to about thirty metres. I was looking out for the red Black Deep buoy, which I expected to see very soon on our starboard side. I was becoming increasingly worried that it wasn't appearing when it should, but I thought that it was because the fog was too thick. While I was poised with the horn and looking hard to starboard for Black Deep, Bob was helming with great intensity. Although we were already motoring quite slowly, he suddenly felt compelled to reduce our speed to tick over and, within seconds of doing so, the Black Deep buoy appeared directly on our nose. Fortunately, we were going slowly enough to be able to turn sharply to starboard and narrowly avoid it, but then the depth showed that we only had two metres under the keel. We were clearly now over the edge of the Black Deep sandbank, which the big, red metal buoy was there to mark. We skirted the buoy and turned rapidly back to port. It had been a really narrow escape. We were so lucky not to have crashed into it and been holed, which might have necessitated abandoning to the life raft in the middle of the Thames estuary in thick fog.

We were horrified and completely baffled as to why Black Deep ended up in front of us when it should have been well to the side. We were in possession of the most recently published 2012 chart but – although we thought we were bang up to date – we eventually discovered that the buoy had been moved only a couple of weeks previously due to the sandbank having shifted. Apparently, they move the buoys regularly so it was a salutary lesson in taking nothing for granted when it comes to anything to do with sailing.

The tussle with the Black Deep buoy was our second near miss, the first one being with the mad Danish Lady in the Outer Hebrides. We were now nearly home and dry and, despite our most recent scary experience, optimistic that we'd had our fill of near collision situations forever and that things didn't always happen in threes. Eventually, the fog cleared and we consoled ourselves with a hot sausage sandwich and coffee, and carried on unscathed to Ramsgate. We decided that the Thames estuary would never be our cruising ground of choice.

We were relieved to arrive in Ramsgate in one piece, and spent a long afternoon exploring. The last time I'd been to Ramsgate was a bit of an emotional blur. We were in the process of moving to Belgium to live and I was driving over with our two daughters to join Bob, who was already installed there. We'd arrived at the port, only to be refused entry on to the ferry to Ostend because we had a hamster (called Scrabble) with us and didn't have the relevant papers. We had two goldfish as well but they didn't count as livestock, and in any case, being fish, would probably have been able to make their own way across. I had in fact tried to be responsible and had spent many long hours phoning different organisations to find out how to legally transport small pets abroad and what documents we would need. Everyone I spoke to seemed not to know what to do. It was a customs officer in Dover who had eventually said that, although he didn't know what the procedure was either, I should just go for it and not worry.

It was his fault, then, that I was sitting in the car in Ramsgate on a Sunday with two wailing and distraught young daughters in the back, wondering what on earth to do. It's not easy to find an emergency vet on a Sunday in a small seaside town but we did find one. He said he knew nothing about documents either (wailing sound getting louder by the minute) but, eventually, with a stroke of genius, offered personally to look after Scrabble in his 'five-star animal menagerie' and write to the girls regularly to let them know how he was getting on. They would also be able to visit whenever they wanted. I wanted to press huge amounts of money into his hands in gratitude. What a marvellous man! As were now walking round the streets of Ramsgate for the second time, I wondered whether we should pay Scrabble a visit but decided that it might be too disruptive for him. He would be about seventeen by now.

Despite my limited previous experience of Ramsgate, I thought it looked quite different from seventeen years ago, but then we had been there on a Sunday and I wasn't in the best of moods. The streets were now perky and bright, and there were lots of quirky and characterful people around. It was Bethnal Green, Bohemia, Trinidad and a refined Georgian seaside resort all rolled into one. The street that frames the harbour was buzzing with life, restaurants and bars, and the tables and chairs spilled out from the open frontages on to the pavements. The bustling harbour was full of all sorts of boats and a large number of support vessels serving the wind farms under construction in the area. There were pound shops galore, and we bought some plastic Union Jack bunting to adorn *Bella Rosa* on her final leg through the Solent. I'd never been in a pound shop before and had to restrain myself from going berserk. The bunting was only 99p.

In the evening, we went to a brilliant fish and chip shop called Eddie Gilbert's. You could choose whether you had chips fried in lard or vegetable fat. We'd never come across that before – even in the Magpie Café – but the implication was that some people don't just come to Eddie Gilbert's to boost their Omega 3 reserves. I was tempted to ask if they could fry mine in organic hemp oil but didn't want to risk getting thrown out. We'd wondered how rough Ramsgate would be during a typical evening but, on returning to *Bella Rosa* from the heart of downtown Ramsgate after dinner, we noticed that it seemed a lot less threatening than it did in the pound shop during the day. The local, thrifty, pension-aware granny Mafia were probably all in bed by then.

A Day Off in Ramsgate

We intended our full day off in Ramsgate to be as lazy as possible. Apart from me doing the passage planning for the Ramsgate to Eastbourne trip, we just went to Waitrose and poked our heads around the door of the local yacht club overlooking the harbour. The Royal Temple Yacht Club welcomes visitors and so we thought we would take full advantage of their hospitality and go and watch Andy Murray versus Tsonga on the big, plasma TV in the bar in the afternoon. After that, it was to be an early night because we needed to catch the early west-going tide to Eastbourne.

Ramsgate to Eastbourne

Ramsgate was an experience we wouldn't have missed for anything, and we were sorry to be leaving without having tried out the karaoke and the jazz bar, going to the folk festival and visiting the Spitfire museum. We resolved to go back one day, but by car.

It made such a change having no restrictions on our next leg to Eastbourne. All we needed was the tide going in the same direction as we were. With a fair tide, we would be able to virtually surf the whole way there. Despite the grey clouds, we could see the coast of France in the distance, and were almost tempted to turn the boat to 180 degrees to pay a quick visit. On other occasions, we may well have done that, but the prospect of a proper bed and a hot bath was beginning to beckon quite strongly. We passed quite close to the white cliffs of Dover but didn't expect to see any bluebirds as, apparently, they are an American invention to make the song sound more colourful. "There are seagulls over the grey cliffs of Dover" doesn't have quite the same ring to it.

The English Channel is one of the busiest shipping channels in the world, and we were running nicely parallel to it. The main shipping lanes run straight down the centre and ferries cross at right angles from ports on either side of the channel. It's only twenty-two miles across at its narrowest point, which is between Dover and Calais. Earlier that day, I'd spotted a pilot boat, which had 'Channel Swim Support Boat' painted in bold letters on its side. Dover to Calais was no doubt the most popular route for channel swimmers because it was the shortest distance and, for us, being able to actually see France made the idea of swimming there almost attractive. Maybe that could be a future challenge when we tired of sailing, we wondered, but only briefly!

On the negative side, swimming twenty-two miles non-stop was one thing, but the other major considerations were having to dodge endless cargo ships, being swept off course by strong tides, being stung by hordes of jellyfish and being poisoned by raw sewage. To cap it all, in order to qualify as an authentic channel swimmer, you weren't even allowed to wear a wetsuit. I crossed the idea firmly off my 'what to do next after the circumnavigation' list.

We knew we would be passing Dungeness at some point in the journey but couldn't see anything in the distance that resembled it. This was a place we'd heard about many times, and my mental picture of it was of a large rugged promontory that rose majestically out of the sea; a bit like Portland Bill. We viewed the flat coastline through the binoculars and were puzzled by what looked like some solid-looking structures poking up from the open sea a few miles in front of us. The closer we got, the more puzzled we became. There was no wind farm or oil platform east of Dungeness marked on our charts, and we didn't know whether we could sail between the 'structures' and the land or whether we should sail round the outside of them, whatever they were. We couldn't work out what on earth we were dealing with so resorted to phoning the coastguard to ask. They assured us that there was nothing out there and were equally puzzled, until, during the conversation, it dawned on us that it must be Dungeness power station and it was connected to the mainland by a long, flat promontory that we just couldn't see. The coastguard officer we were speaking to was very polite as we made our apologies and, although we couldn't hear any stifled laughter, the office staff must have had hysterics after they'd put down the phone. What a couple of daft twits! How did we ever get to be in charge of anything, let alone a boat?

Eastbourne marina is called the Sovereign marina and is situated a few miles down the coast from Eastbourne town. It's one of those new developments with attitude, and is a high-living and shopping opportunity, boating and cinema complex and cosmetic dentistry experience all rolled into one. In the marina brochure, it states that there are at least three cosmetic dentists on site. If Bob had known that back in mid April, we might have gone anticlockwise.

If we were ever to have a permanent berth in the Sovereign marina, it would be fitting for Bob to wear a gold ingot and all that goes with that particular look. I'd have to wear white jeans with rhinestones on the derrière, and an assortment of other bling. Apparently, there was a bar in the marina that had a massive TV in it so we were hoping to be able to watch the tennis the following afternoon, so long as they didn't have it switched over to *Cash in The Attic*.

A Day Off in Eastbourne

Our mission on our day off in Eastbourne was to watch the men's tennis finals with Andy Murray, and we'd discovered that there were in fact two places in the marina complex with big screen TVs. One was in the slightly rough-looking bar close to the water, and the other was at the resident yacht club that 'welcomed visiting yachtsmen'. Bob was fully qualified to enter the yacht club by virtue of being not only a man but also by being off a yacht and a visitor, so he went to the yacht club and I went to the bar, whose only entry stipulations were to be over eighteen. Actually, that wasn't true at all. We both started off in the bar and both ended up in the yacht club. I think they let me in without question because of the beard and eyepatch I'd been sporting since Peterhead.

Murray didn't win, which was a shame because it would have been so good for British morale for that to happen in the same year as Britain hosting the Olympics and the Queen's Diamond Jubilee. Still, it was two out of three positive things.

We were by now only two passages away from the end of our amazing adventure. The penultimate passage would take us as far as Itchenor, near Chichester, where we would meet up with our friends Sue and Richard on their boat, *Violet*. After that, we would sail to Lymington together, where my parents would come and meet us and – no doubt – we would raise a glass or two to the real heroine of the trip: *Bella Rosa*, the Wonder Boat.

We'd met four other 'roundBritainers' on our trip:

we'd met *Miss Amelia* in Arklow; *Alize* was still pottering around the Thames estuary; *Jambo* had already arrived in Eastbourne; and *Dawn Treader*, who we'd shared some significant time with, was now only one port behind us in Ramsgate. The end was nigh!

Eastbourne to Itchenor

I was wrong about the rhinestones. The ultimate accessory in Eastbourne marina complex was a bull terrier and a plethora of complex tattoos. We said our farewells and ventured forth on our penultimate passage to Itchenor and to our home territory: the Solent.

It was exactly twelve weeks since we'd left Lymington on 16 April. We could see the pale grey shadow of the Isle of Wight as we sailed south of Selsey Bill and past the Owers shoals. Ted Heath's nephew had been killed on the shoals in gales in 1973 when he was sailing *Morning Cloud*. They were a dangerous hazard in many states of tide, and were not to be messed with. The conditions for us were less challenging than when *Morning Cloud* had been sailing but we still chose to go south of the shoals to be on the safe side. It had been touching a Force 6 when we'd set off that morning, which is known as a 'yachtsman's gale', but throughout the rest of the day it remained a consistent Force 4 to 5, which was still quite vigorous but not too demanding.

Fortunately, the conditions were perfect for us to cross the shallow sandbar up into Chichester harbour and on to meet Sue and Richard in Itchenor. We arrived in Itchenor at 6 o'clock in the evening to the warmest of welcomes. *Violet* was sporting a 'Welcome Home' banner, and Sue and Richard had a bottle of Union-Jack-clad, ice-cold champagne at the ready. *Bella Rosa* (the Wonder Boat) and *Violet* (the Super Boat) were to be rafted together for the night on a big, fat, white mooring buoy that could apparently accommodate up to ten medium-sized yachts if necessary. Two boats were plenty, we thought.

Once all the appropriate lines were fixed, we joined Sue and Richard on *Violet*'s deck to sit in the evening sun sipping champagne and nibbling crisps before dinghying off to the pub for dinner. We hadn't seen each other for three months, so there was so much catching up to do, and boat talk was right at the top of the agenda.

The following day, we would be sailing back to Lymington and would finally close the circle around mainland Britain. *Bella Rosa* would be clad in Union Jack bunting, but we were keeping our fingers crossed that it wouldn't rain as the bargain bunting was only made of paper. It was a strange thought that our big adventure was all going to come to an end the next day.

Our Last Leg: Itchenor to Lymington

The following morning, on our very last day, we climbed back on to *Violet* for our last circumnavigation breakfast and to stoke up for the grand re-entry.

We couldn't leave Itchenor until just after midday to ensure that we had enough height of tide safely to cross the sandbar at the estuary entrance. We also wanted it to be as close to high water as possible when we arrived back in Lymington. A high water arrival meant that it would be easier for my parents to negotiate the ramp to the pontoons, which would rise up with the tide and be fairly flat. We left Itchenor harbour in south-west winds, which were gusting to 24 knots. This meant that we would have to tack our way back up the Solent because we couldn't sail directly into the wind. We zigzagged our way towards our destination and felt the wind increase even more as we rounded the entrance to the Medina River at Cowes. During the final couple of hours, it was beginning to gust to a Force 7, with grey skies and sporadic rain showers. It was supposed to be summer, and yet we were clad in full, foul weather gear and our last sail was turning out to be 'full on' and highly invigorating. Sailing in a sunny Force 4 with the wind behind us would have been a lovely way to finish, but at least we were sailing and not motoring. We would not have wanted to finish with a whimper.

We could see that my parents were already down on the pontoon taking photos as we chugged along the Lymington River to reclaim our old berth. It was a tough job getting them over the guard rails but they insisted on coming onboard to join us in celebrating our safe arrival with champagne, followed by dinner at the Ship Inn on Lymington Quay. The Owens, who had arrived back in Lymington shortly after us, came over to join us. We were thrilled to have successfully completed our mission but equally sad that our odyssey had finally come to an end. The saddest moment was having to say a temporary goodbye to our trusty and wonderful boat, *Bella Rosa*, who had made it all possible and had kept us safe and sound throughout all manner of things.

FINAL REFLECTIONS

There had been so many facets of our trip round Britain, the most obvious being the challenge of keeping *Bella Rosa* the right way up and pointing in the right direction. Some might have said that we were clueless (and crewless) deciding to circumnavigate Britain but, having managed to sail back from Holland by ourselves, sailed to the Isles of Scilly and back the previous year and spent some time being forced to 'get to know our boat' by Alex, we felt that we had been ready to tackle what was left of the British coastline, which was still pretty much all of it.

We knew that stress-free passages were going to be all about making the right decisions based on the weather, the wind, and the direction and strength of the tides. We were on a mission, so needed to get on when we could, and there were few – if any – days when we felt frustrated that we'd missed good sailing conditions. Timing, we knew, was going to be everything, which would sometimes mean leaving a port in the wee small hours of the morning or else fighting foul tides and missing tidal gates over sandbars or harbour sills.

One of the most satisfying things as we reflected on our experiences was that most of – if not all – our decisions had been the right ones. We'd taken advantage of weather windows when they'd presented themselves, even if it did mean getting up in the dark and setting off in cold, wet weather. A well-timed bacon butty had frequently helped to still the waters of an early start. But we'd also been patient, careful and stayed put when all the information had pointed that way. There were many days when we said to each other, "Glad we're not out there!" and far fewer when we said, "What are we doing here?"

We'd initially agreed that if a Force 6 was mentioned in any forecast we wouldn't leave port. Unfortunately, *Bella Rosa* often had other ideas and refused to be stuck for very long anywhere that didn't have a decent pontoon, a good chandlery and other quality boats to mingle with. With *Bella Rosa*'s unrelenting determination to carry on, we soon realised that it's not possible to sail round Britain within a lifetime without going out in stronger winds at least some of the time.

We had very few dodgy moments, which was a big surprise, considering we were braced for all sorts of problems from bits of the boat dropping off, the engine packing in, personal injuries, being unexpectedly stuck in a Force 10 or even running out of Fox's Classic biscuits. The closest we ever got to a potential sinking were the two near collisions: one with the rampant Danish lady; and the other with the inconveniently positioned Black Deep buoy in the Thames estuary. If we'd had to choose which one of the two was going to take us down, we would have opted for the Danish lady. Then at least there would have been someone else to blame. It would be hard to sue a static red buoy.

As for disappointments, we struggle to think of any, but the Cornish pasties we bought in Newlyn to eat during our night sail were an absolute travesty. We were also under the impression that the prevailing winds in Britain were meant to be south-westerly. In reality, the prevailing winds frequently came from wherever we happened to be facing, which made the sailing much harder work. We were expecting it to be cold but not quite so relentlessly icy cold. Sometimes, I did feel quite worn down by the cold but was saved by my trusty hot-water bottle and having taken several hundred thermal vests with me. A big thanks is due to Marks & Spencer for running a three-for-two offer just before we set sail.

We were thrilled to have sailed to the Outer Hebrides – as it certainly hadn't been in our original game plan – but, unfortunately, we didn't manage to set foot on Harris because we didn't want to risk leaving *Bella Rosa* anchored alone in strong winds. She might have done a runner.

Our list of highlights is endless, the biggest one being that we actually circumnavigated the whole of mainland Britain, enjoyed every single minute of it and had the most tremendous adventure. Every single day brought forth a new challenge and the chance to reflect deeply on life in one of the most natural and unspoiled of environments – the sea. The simplicity of life on the water was truly liberating, and being constantly in the company of so much glorious wildlife from dolphins to puffins was awesome.

Every day, even just stepping up into the cockpit with a morning cup of tea in hand, we were able to appreciate nature in its rawest form. The sea can be wild, isolated, hostile and dangerous but it can also be the most soothing of environments, a place of unadulterated beauty and a refuge from the niggling details of everyday life onshore. There are no traffic jams. It's a private wilderness and yet can be a stone's throw away from the security of civilisation.

Before we left, there were so many places in Britain that we'd never visited, which was one of the main reasons why we wanted to do the trip in the first place. Travelling by boat, we'd been able to see so much more of our island home than we'd ever envisaged, from the more affluent areas in the south to the struggling fishing ports in the north and east. We came across so many deliciously pretty tourist towns like Fowey and Tobermory, and the remote but strong communities on the islands of Mull and the Orkneys. We stopped in sophisticated marinas in big towns like Newcastle and Dun Laoghaire, tiny fishing harbours like Arbroath, and big working fishing harbours like Lochinver. We'd picked up mooring buoys in places like the Kyles of Bute and Otter Ferry, and anchored in out-of-the-way places like Inverary and Canna Island.

The variety of terrain was vast but the common feature of all these places was how interested, encouraging, kind, friendly and helpful the people were, no matter what their circumstances. We had the warmest of welcomes from so many locals, and met some of the loveliest of harbour masters and marina staff. We came to the conclusion that – contrary to what the press lead you to believe – the British people, **all** the British people, from every corner of this island, really do put the 'Great' into Great Britain, and I think we both came back with a strong sense of being proud to be British and feeling so lucky to live in Britain.

Up until this point, I haven't allowed myself any postscripts to this book, but I feel I have to make an exception over the Scottish referendum. Since completing the book, the Scottish people have rejected the opportunity to take their country out of the United Kingdom. I am so relieved and passionately happy that they took this decision. Neil Oliver, historian and presenter of *Coast*, has written eloquently about this and, to describe my own feelings, I can do no better than quote his open letter to the Scottish people ahead of the referendum:

I have no economic argument to make. Frankly, I am sick and tired of hearing people argue the toss about the pound, pensions and the rest. I am voting No because, for me, the offering by the Yes camp lacks nobility and humanity.

Having spent years working on the television series, Coast, I think it's fair to say I've seen as much of this United Kingdom of ours as anyone else living here. It's a project that has changed my life in several ways. It has certainly caused me to fall in love with the place – the whole place. Circumnavigate these islands as I have, as often as I have, and one thing above all becomes clear: the national boundaries within are invisible and therefore meaningless.

People living in a fishing town in Cornwall have more in common with the inhabitants of a fishing town in Fife than either population has with the folk of a town in the Midlands. They have a shared experience and a common history of coping with lives shaped by the sea. The coast is another country – the fifth country – and it unites us and binds us like the hem of a garment.

The differences that are discernible as you travel around Britain are regional ones – made of accents and architecture, geology and geography. I am all in favour of people having the power to make decisions about their own patch but I am utterly opposed to the idea of breaking centuries old bonds in order to make that happen.

Circumnavigating Britain is without a doubt a challenge and, as with all challenges, there is an accompanying camaraderie with others who are embarking on the same thing. A particularly special moment for us was when we were finally setting off to round Cape Wrath and we found that we were in the company of *Dawn Treader*. Not only was it reassuring that they must have done the same calculations and had come to the same conclusions about the best time to leave, but there also seemed to be an unspoken bond unmatched by anything else we'd ever done. We were setting off with similar feelings of excitement and trepidation, had the same lofty goal and were keen to watch out for each other with the hope that each of us would achieve what we set out to do.

As for our own situation, despite living together in a tiny space for twenty-four hours a day for three months, we had rare moments of discord. I think it was the knowledge that here was an opportunity to have the experience of a lifetime, and we weren't going to let any bad humour taint it in any way. We were continually excited about what we were doing, and thoroughly enjoyed working it all out together. Even after thirty-four years, when you embark on something new together you not only learn more about yourself but more about each other. We would agree that what we both learnt was all favourable. We were 'Team Tyrrell' and having a tremendous time.

There's so much more that could be said, but I'm going to finish with a quote:

"Cruising has two main pleasures. One is to go out into wider waters from a sheltered place. The other is to go into a sheltered place from wider waters".
Howard Bloomfield, *Sailing to the Sun*

Thanks

The most important person who deserves my thanks is my husband Bob, who eventually agreed to accompany me on our three-month escapade and, despite being male, was 100% gracious in accepting my position as skipper. His support was constant, his role as second in command exemplary, and his creations with the Remoska sublime. We now have some extraordinary shared memories and an extra bond in our relationship that we didn't even know was out there to be had.

One of the most heart-warming aspects of our challenge was how much amazing support we had from our family and friends. We had huge encouragement, help and advice from many quarters well before we set off. We were waved off and welcomed back by my parents. Our daughters, Gracie and Sophie, sent some 'Good Luck' balloons and a bottle of champagne to have whenever we felt we needed it, and phoned us regularly. The balloons stayed inflated in the front cabin for several weeks. Frances was so constant in her support that she could well have been on the boat with us. The 'Randoms' gave us a great, Union-Jack-themed send-off party. Mark very kindly set up the blog for us, which turned out to be such an enjoyable and fulfilling thing for us to do as well as enabling us to get a regular following and post photos. We had Vivien heroically holding the fort for us back home, checking the house regularly for deluges and unexpected acts of God. Our dependable friend, Stuart, looked after our dog Bonnie for us, as well as sending the post on to various marinas around Britain. Our next door neighbours, David and Annie, checked through the curtains regularly that we didn't have squatters. We had endless advice and encouragement from our expert sailing friends, Janene, Jules and Mike. We especially liked the comment from Jules when asked whether he thought we should tackle Cape Wrath, which was "How bad could it be?" Jules has sailed in 70 knots of wind around the Falkland Islands.

Susan, Angela, Vivien and Alison sent long emails so that I wouldn't feel 'out of sight, out of mind'. Louise and Peter came up to see us in Tarbert to check that we hadn't gone bonkers, and selflessly helped us check out a fish restaurant there. We had constant newsy emails from so many friends keeping us up to date with what was happening back in Bath. We had great recommendations about where to go and which restaurants to visit from friends who knew an area well. Chris was watching us on various webcams and doing screenshots of us coming into various ports. My sister Sue printed off the blog every few days and sent it to my parents, who don't own a computer, so that they were able to keep up with our exploits. Sue and Richard not only appeared the day before we left with a couple of customised 'Bella Rosa Round Britain 2012' sailing caps but also met up with us at the end of the trip to sail back to Lymington with us. Melanie and John provided us with a 'boat bag' of necessary equipment, without which we would never have got beyond Milford Haven. I'm thinking particularly of the Laughter hand wash, which was a daily reminder to keep as cheerful as possible at all times and was essential to our morale. It was this strong, warm wave of friendship and support that stayed firmly under us every single nautical mile we travelled.

Photo Journal
Throughout all Manner of Things

Newlyn Harbour

Penzance after the Storm

About to sail round Land's End

The Amiable Alex

Dale at Dusk Waiting to Cross the Irish Sea

Dun Laoghaire Marina

The Forty Foot

SEVERE CAKE WARNING
RED ALERT

The Promenade Cafe in Dun Laoghaire

Calm Weather in Ardglass

Look out for the O'Somalies

Still in Charge

The Giant's Causeway

Bushmills Bob

With Louise and Peter in Tarbert

The Kyles of Bute

Bella Rosa Anchored Outside Inveraray

Crinan

Emerging the Other Side of the Crinan Canal

Canna Island

Canna Sunset

Coastal Turmoil

Mallaig at Night

Slain's Castle

Arbroath

Dawn Treader On the Way From Lochinver to Kinlochbervie

Spinks's Smokies

Whitby and the Captain Cook Cruise

Whitby Abbey

Sunrise Near Grimsby

Bella Rosa After an Engine Service

Bella Rosa Looking Pleased with Herself

Harwich Town Quay

Jules, Bob and Janine having coffee and cake in Suffolk

Thames Barges On The River Stour

Leaving The River Stour and Heading For the Thames Estuary in The Early Hours

Ramsgate

Ramsgate Harbour

Eastbourne Marina Entrance

Chugging Down The Lymington River on Our Last Day

The End
Throughout all Manner of Things

www.ingramcontent.com/pod-product-compliance
Lightning Source LLC
Chambersburg PA
CBHW042123100526
44587CB00026B/4167